TRIED IN THE FIRE

McDougal & Associates
Servants of Christ and stewards of the mysteries of God

TRIED IN THE FIRE

by

Dr. Gwendolyn L. Washington

Unless otherwise noted, all Scripture quotations are from the Authorized King James Version of the Bible. References marked "NAS" are from the New American Standard Version of the Bible, copyright © 1960, 1962, 1963, 1968, 1971, 1972, 1973, 1975, 1977 by the Lockman Foundation, La Habra, California.

TRIED IN THE FIRE
Copyright © 2007—by Gwendolyn L. Washington
ALL RIGHTS RESERVED

No part of this book may be reproduced or transmitted in any form or by any means, electronic or mechanical, including photocopying, recording, or by any information retrieval system.

Original cover design by Lara York
zoecreationgrafx@bellsouth.net

Published by:

McDougal & Associates
www.thepublishedword.com

McDougal & Associates is dedicated to the spreading of the Gospel of Jesus Christ to as many people as possible in the shortest time possible.

ISBN 13: 978-0-9786332-0-2
ISBN 10: 0-9786332-0-2

Printed in the United States of America
For Worldwide Distribution

DEDICATION

To my oldest sister/mother: Mrs. Fedie J. Clemmons

My Daughters: Fedie Renee Redd and Patricia Lynn Redd, Eileen Connelly and, Beverly Connolly-Copeland

My God Children: Nichele Rochford-Boakye, Lisa Griggs, Gwen Renee Rodas, Missionary Jamerilla Fyffe, Debra Evora, Minister Ron Miller, Elder Jerry and Mrs. Debra Brown, Minister Edward and Michelle Harris, Mr. and Mrs. Phillip Evelyn, the Clark sisters: Evangelist Dorinda Clark-Cole, Mrs. Karen Clark-Sheard, Elbernita "Twinkie" Clark, and Jackie Clark-Chisholm

My Baby Grands: Kira ShaNay, Kason Delaney, Fedie Dominique, Danasia Jamani, Danielle Jenee, Keldin Resean and Bryanna Jhomae (God-Granddaughter)

My Baby Great Grands: Kalin, Kamyia-Lynn and Kailyn Delaney

My Special Family: Superintendent Tommie A. and Mrs. Doris Murphy and my special baby grands, Trevira Nicole and Ericka Lanee Murphy

In Loving Memory of: my daddy, Elder Henry T. Gandy, Sr.; my loving mother, Mother Delia C. Gandy; and my husband, Bishop F.D. Washington, and my mother and mentor, Evangelist Elsie Shaw

ACKNOWLEDGMENTS

First of all, I would like to thank God, the Father of our Lord Jesus Christ, who by His infinite love and mercy has brought me through a life of being *Tried in the Fire*. Please know that my life is still coming together, as the apostle Paul declared:

> *For we know in part and we prophesy in part; but when the perfect comes, the partial will be done away.*   1 Corinthians 13:9-10, NAS

> *And we know that all things work together for good to them that love God, to them who are the called according to his purpose.*   Romans 8:28

Second, I thank Him for allowing me to be born of godly parents: Elder Henry Thomas Gandy, Sr. and Mother Delia C. Gandy.

Third, I wish to honor our church and its leaders:

I'm very thankful that I was honored to be under the ministry of our founder, the late Bishop Charles Harrison Mason. He prayed for me and spoke beautiful words into my life. I love our church, the **Church of God in Christ,** and deem it important to honor and respect the position of our most powerfully anointed leaders:

Our Presiding Bishop, G.E. Patterson, and his beautiful wife, Lady Louise Patterson: Thank you! Every morning, as I kneel in prayer, I never fail to pray for you. I love you, and thank God for the respect and favor that was rendered to me, while my husband was alive, and also after he went to be with the Lord. May the Lord continue to bless and enrich your lives is my prayer.

The Members of the General Board and their wives: Bishop and Mrs. Charles E. Blake, 1st Vice President, Bishop and Mrs. J.N. Haynes, 2nd Vice President; Bishop and Mrs. W.W. Hamilton, Secretary; Bishop and Mrs. Roy L.H. Winbush,

Assistant Secretary; Bishop and Mrs. Chandler David Owens, Former Presiding Bishop; Bishop and Mrs. P.A. Brooks, Bishop and Mrs. Samuel L. Green, Jr.; Bishop and Mrs. Leroy R. Anderson; Bishop and Mrs. Nathaniel W. Wells; Bishop George D. McKinney; and Bishop J.W. Macklin

The National Board of Bishops and their wives: Represented by Bishop John H. Sheard, Chairman, and Mrs. Daisy Sherman, Chairlady

The General Council of Pastors and Elders and their wives: Represented by Superintendent Derrick W. Hutchins, Chairman.

The General Assembly: Represented by Bishop James Oglethorpe Patterson, Chairman

The General Supervisor of Women, Mother Willie Mae Rivers: I pause here to honor and respect you for being an example and mother to me and other women in this church, because you have spoken into my life. I want to say thank you! What a mighty woman of God you are! My prayers for you ascend before the throne of God each and every morning. May the God of peace be with you. I love you, Mom!

Special Honor To Bishop and Mrs. James Gaylord, Teaneck, New Jersey, who have been there for me since the death of my husband. Through many of my trying times, they have stepped up to the plate. Bishop Gaylord is also the sponsor of this book.

To **Bishop and Mrs. James C. Austin**, who took me under the arms of their For Christ Ministry when souls were at stake and appointed me supervisor over that powerful ministry sponsored by St. Luke Church of God in Christ. Bishop Austin took Bibles, computers, office equipment and money and built churches in that country. I rate them five star all the way.

My Jurisdictional Prelate, Bishop Leroy Jackson Woolard, and Mother Dorothy Woolard and my Jurisdictional Supervisor of Woman: Mother Mary Love Green: Thank you for sharing and caring.

The Department of Women and its Supervisors, especially Mother Barbara McCoo Lewis of Los Angeles, California: Thank you for your love and caring. For you, I am praying.

Special thanks to pastors across the country who have opened the doors of their churches for me to minister: Bishop Chandler D. and Mother Shirley Owens, Church of God in Christ Family (Marietta, Georgia); Bishop and Mrs. Jacob Cohen, AM Cohen Temple Family (Miami, Florida); Bishop James C. and Lady Vernesta Austin and Elder Ralph and Lady Arlene Land, St. Luke Church Family (Chicago, Illinois); Bishop James and Lady Josephine Gaylord, Kelly Temple Church Family (New York, New York); Bishop Frank O. and Dr. Juliette White, Zion Cathedral Church Family (Freeport, New York); Bishop Charles Brewer, Trinity Temple Church Family (New Haven, Connecticut); Bishop and Mrs. Norman Prescott, Trinity Temple Church Family (Montclair, New Jersey); Bishop Jerry Macklin, Glad Tidings Church Family (Heyward, California); Dr. Lawyer John and Dr. Faye Ellis Butler, Salvation Restoration Christian Center Church Family (Brooklyn, New York); Superintendent Dr. Willie and Dr. Gwendolyn Robinson, Glorious Temple Church Family (Brooklyn, New York); Bishop John and Pastor ViCurtis Little, Capitol Temple Church Family (Washington, D.C.); Dr. Lauren and Lady Barbara Mann, Pentecostal Temple Church (Pittsburgh, Pennsylvania); Apostle Reginald and Pastor Emma White, Gospel Lighthouse Ministries (Wadesboro, North Carolina); Dr. and Mrs. Jerry Burns, Open Door Church Family (Brooklyn, New York); Bishop and Mrs. B.R. Benbow and Daughter, Mrs. Lillie Smarr, Eighty-Eighth Street Church Family (Los Angeles, California); Superintendent and Mrs. Ron Surrey, New Mt. Olive Church Family (New Britain, Connecticut); Dr. and Mrs. Isaac Patrick, Gospel Light Church Family (Santa Ana, California); Bishop and Mrs. Benjamin Collins (Savannah, Georgia); Bishop Larry Shaw, Missionary Denise Kimble, Missionary Patricia Patterson, Evangelist Barbara Williams, Mother Bernice Rivers, Full Gospel Tabernacle Church Family (Hinesville, Georgia); Pastor and Mrs. Mark Vereen (Richmond, Virginia); Bishop and Mrs. Lee Gaddie, Missionary Gigi Cooper (Houston, Texas); Pastor William and Missionary Stephanie Meredith, Mother Mary Meredith, Meredith Temple Church (Columbus, Ohio); Pastor Darryl Grant, Mother Nancy Grant, Kingdom Builders Church Family (Charlotte, North Carolina); Apostle Regina Cherry, Solid Rock Church Family (Rock Hill, South Carolina); Pastor Viola Blackburn (Rock Hill, South Carolina); Pastor and Mrs. Daryl Johnson, True Way Church Family (Charlotte, North Carolina); Bishop and Mrs. Leroy J. Woolard, Pentecostal Temple Church Family (Plymouth, North Carolina); Superintendent and Mrs. Frankie Davis, Mt. Zion Church Family (Charlotte, North Carolina), Bishop and Mrs. Matthew Williams and the Brown Memorial Church Family (Tampa, Florida), Bishop and Mrs. Bobby Henderson, Anointed Word Ministry (Atlanta, Georgia), Bishop David and Mrs. Cordelia Wallace, Agape Cathedral (Brooklyn, New York), Ambassador Melvin C. Walker (Hempstead, New York), Superintendent and Mrs. Robert L. Madison (Brooklyn, New York), and Washington Temple Church and my church family (This was my church home for more than thirty-eight years.)

Contents

Foreword by Dr. Julia L. White 10
Foreword by Bishop James Gaylord 12

Introduction 15

1. His Quiver Full 19
2. You Formed My Inward Parts 25
3. I Put Away Childish Things 35
4. To Give You an Expected End 49
5. I Will Bless Thee 63
6. They Hated Knowledge 81
7. Speak, for Thy Servant Heareth 97
8. His Praise in Jerusalem 105
9. Free Indeed 113
10. I Have Chosen You 129
11. I Have Put My Words in Your Mouth 143
12. Plenteous in Mercy 151
13. Think It Not Strange 161
14. The Lord Your God Is with You 179
15. God Is Not Unrighteous to Forget Your Work 199
16. I Will Restore You to Health 207
17. He Sent His Word and Healed Them 213
18. With His Stripes We Are Healed 221

The Healing Scriptures 225
Ministry Page 240

Foreword by
Dr. Juliet L. White

Dr. Gwendolyn Washington is a gift to the Christian community, as well as a portrait of inspiration among all those who encounter her creative and effective evangelistic style. Carefully following the details of our Savior's earthly ministry, the body of information covered by her research, her literary framework and, above all, her hands-on approach to soul-wining, make publications such as this an indispensable tool at all levels of missionary fieldwork.

Beyond her success as a true-hearted woman of God, as the surviving spouse of the late and honorable hero of Gospel proclamation, the Bishop Frederick D. Washington, Mrs. Washington introduces to this work the unique benefit and passion of a first lady's perspective. It is within these combined capacities that I have come to know, respect, and admire Dr. Washington for the worthy contribution she continues to offer to this, our holy profession. The ideas formulated in this work, therefore, summarize an abundant lifetime testimony of love, patience, and anointed insight. It is precisely these refreshing godly virtues—at work among the saints—which make her genuinely herself.

Dr. Juliet L. White
Elect Lady, Zion Cathedral COGIC
Freeport, New York

Forward by Bishop James Gaylord

I had the privilege of meeting Sister Gwendolyn Washington a few years ago, as we had something in common—winning souls for Christ. We worked the fields together, gathering in the harvest, and I concluded that she really loved God, and her desire was to keep the charge given her by our Lord Jesus Christ in Mark 16:15: *"Go ye into all the world, and preach the gospel to every creature."*

The Word of God states in Revelation 3:18: *"I counsel thee to buy of me gold tried in the fire, that thou mayest be rich."* Because of the many testimonies charged to her account, it is altogether fitting that a book should be written. I believe that this book will go where some men cannot go, and through the reading of its pages, decisions will be made to follow in the footsteps of Jesus.

I agree with the publisher that this is a story that needs to be told, and that the many lessons in its content will help the younger generations and, indeed, people of all generations. I also agree with him that this is anointed material and that, because the contents of its pages is scriptural, it give this material authenticity. I have no doubt that this book was orchestrated by God and that it will accomplish the things He has ordained it to do.

My theme song is God is calling me to a higher place of praise, and my prayer is that *Tried in the Fire* by Gwendolyn Washington will be received and read, sharing freely part of her story and much of God's amazing grace, thus bringing her into that higher place of praise.

Bishop James Gaylord
Kelly Temple Church of God in Christ, Inc.
Jurisdictional Prelate of Eastern New York

I counsel thee to buy of me gold TRIED IN THE FIRE, that thou mayest be rich.
        Revelation 3:18, Emphasis Added

But he knoweth the way that I take: when he hath tried me, I shall come forth AS GOLD.   Job 23:10, Emphasis Added

Behold, I will send my messenger, and he shall prepare the way before me: ... But who may abide the day of his coming? and who shall stand when he appeareth? for he is like A REFINER'S FIRE, and like fullers' soap: and he shall sit as a refiner and purifier of silver.   Malachi 3:1-3, Emphasis Added

Introduction

For many years now, I've been promising to write this book. It's purpose is not to glorify me, but to let people know that when we give ourselves to God and become saved, that's the beginning of victory for our lives.

Before I accepted Christ as my personal Savior, I can never remember a time when life was easy. I was in and out of all sorts of difficult situations, when I was still young and living at home, and this continued after I had left home and was on my own. Nothing changed ... until I said yes to the Lord. Then everything changed.

I promised the Lord I would write this as a witness to the fact that He has a master plan for every one of our lives, and that master plan extends from earliest childhood right on through our adult lives. Hold on to His promises, dear child of God, for He will never fail you.

For instance, because the Lord promised to save your children and your family, take Him at His Word. He has said:

> *But they that wait upon the L*ORD *shall renew their strength; they shall mount up with wings as eagles; they shall run, and not be weary; they shall walk, and not faint.* Isaiah 40:31

Like many, I went through a lot trying to find love in this world, and I had to learn the hard way that God *is* love. We can either receive Him and be blessed, or we can reject Him and be cursed. In my case, I ran from Him for many years. But when your family is praying for you, as mine was, it makes all the difference in the world.

Eventually, I was given an ultimatum from God Himself: "Either give your heart to Me and live, or reject Me and die young." I chose not to shorten my life because of ignorance, but to count the cost and go with Jesus. And so, I surrendered my all to Him.

I'm so glad that the Father drew me to His Son, for Jesus Himself said:

> *No man can come to me, except the Father which hath sent me draw him.*   John 6:44

It was only at the point of my surrender to Christ that the utter emptiness I had experienced for thirty years was eased. I had thought love was to be found in a man, and I had searched for it there. In the end, I found that all I needed was Jesus. As the song goes:

> *He satisfies;*
> *My joy He supplies.*
> *Life would be worthless without Him;*
> *All things in Jesus I've found.*

Because I said yes to the Lord, and sold out to Him, He has brought me through many trying situations. I've suffered many afflictions in this life, but, as He promised, the Lord has delivered me out of them all.

There's always a reason for everything we suffer. The Lord has to prepare us, and we must be *"tried in the fire,"* so that we can come forth *"as gold."*

Today, I urge you to yield to the Master Potter. Let Him mold and make you after His will. Be sure you are waiting in His presence, yielded and still. He will do the rest.

As for me, I have now traveled to many nations, taking God's Word to others, and I will share some of those travels with you in this book. As I have traveled, God's favor has accompanied me, His hand has guided me, and His anointing has empowered me.

When I got saved, the first thing I wanted to do was to go to Jerusalem, the Holy City. I've now been there twice and was baptized in the River Jordan, where the Holy Ghost descended upon me. That was also part of the preparation I needed to be *"meet for the master's use"*:

> *If a man therefore purge himself from these, he shall be a vessel unto honour, sanctified, and meet for the master's use, and prepared unto every good work.*
> 2 Timothy 2:21

Through these pages, dear reader, I want you to discover that you, too, can make it. You are an overcomer, because God is with you. If you will just remain focused and seek Him daily in devotion and prayer, He will bring you through and give you a glorious future.

You must hold fast to your dreams and be positive, doing as the wise Solomon instructed:

> *Trust in the* Lord *with all thine heart; and lean not unto thine own understanding. In all thy ways acknowledge him, and he shall direct thy paths.*
>
> Proverbs 3:5-6

Now, come with me, as I relate to you how I was *Tried in the Fire* and how the Lord has brought me forth *"as gold."*

Gwendolyn Washington
Charlotte, North Carolina

CHAPTER ONE
HIS QUIVER FULL

As arrows are in the hand of a mighty man; so are children of the youth. Happy is the man that hath his quiver full of them: they shall not be ashamed, but they shall speak with the enemies in the gate.

Psalm 127:4-5

Before the foundation of the world, our daddy, Elder Henry T. Gandy, Sr., and our mother, Mother Delia C. Fox-Gandy, were in the plan of God. Before they were in their mother's womb, God knew that they would be conceived, be born, grow up, get saved, get married, and replenish the earth with the Gandy children. God also knew that they would bring each of us up in the grand old Church of God in Christ. There were twelve living children for many years, and now we are ten. Daddy and Mama were not ashamed to have their quiver full of us.

TRIED IN THE FIRE

Daddy pastored a small Church of God in Christ and worked as a cotton linter in the Memphis Cotton Exchange. Mama was a home missionary, and she also ran our busy and active home.

THAT LITTLE HOUSE IN MEMPHIS

> *One of our God's names is El-Shaddai! He is more than enough!*

I can never forget the little house at 2369 Devoy Avenue in the city of Memphis and suburb of Hollywood. I thought it was the biggest house in town, a corner house with hedges around it (where Mama cut her switches). There were also beautiful rose bushes, an apple tree, and two peach trees. There was a very large tree in the back yard that I loved to climb.

Daddy had a printing press downstairs in the basement, and when he wasn't at his day job, he worked down there. He could hear everything happening upstairs, so, we had to walk the line when he was around. He would tap on the ceiling, which meant, "I can hear you; don't make me come up there."

Often, when I'm in Memphis for the annual Convocation of the church, I go back to that neighborhood to reminisce, and when I view the tiny lot where that house sat, I think about Jesus feeding the multitude with just three little fish and five loaves of bread. How did He do that? And how did twelve children live on a tiny forty by eighty lot and think of it as being more than an acre? God's ways are past finding out.

THE PROVISION OF EL-SHADDAI

We always had plenty of food in our house and enough to share. During the Convocation, Mama kept a blind preacher (Elder Riley) at our home. I don't remember exactly where he slept. She would cook a big pot of vegetable soup, so that after the three-day fast preceding the Convocation, she could serve many of the saints who attended from around the country. Where did the food come from? One of our God's names is El-Shaddai. He is more than enough.

We needed El-Shaddai in our home, for I was the sixth child of fifteen. Only fourteen of us lived. Two of those I never knew because they died before I was born. Our parents named us as follows: Altha (she's deceased), Dorothy (she's deceased), Fedie, Sarah (she's deceased), Henry Jr., Gwendolyn, David, Donald, the twins: Edwinor (she's deceased) and Eleanor, Carolyn Lynn, Annette, Evelyn, and Wendell. So, now we're ten.

MAMA AND DADDY WORKED TOGETHER FOR GOOD

Mama, interestingly enough, was the disciplinarian of the family. You would never have known that to meet her. She was a sweet, loving, caring, and powerful woman of God, but knew how to use Daddy's authority. All she had to say, if and when we got too far out of line, was: "Don't make me tell your daddy when he gets home," and we straightened up quickly. We surely didn't want to feel the pain of Daddy's belt, so those few words always got our attention. In this way, Daddy and Mama worked together for good in our family.

They raised us with certain scriptures, believing their promises:

> *Train up a child in the way he should go: and when he is old, he will not depart from it.*   Proverbs 22:6
>
> *He that spareth his rod hateth his son: but he that loveth him chasteneth him betimes.*   Proverbs 13:24
>
> *Withhold not correction from the child: for if thou beatest him with the rod, he shall not die.*
>   Proverbs 23:13
>
> *Foolishness is bound in the heart of a child; but the rod of correction shall drive it far from him.*
>   Proverbs 22:15
>
> *Pride goes before destruction, and an haughty spirit before a fall.*   Proverbs 16:18

Working on the Building

Mama always called us sweet names, like Cake, Pie,

HIS QUIVER FULL

Sugar or Sugar Lump, and she complimented and bragged on us when we had done a good job at anything. But she also knew how to work us over when we were bad. She did it with great purpose and with the future in mind. I could almost hear this song as she disciplined us:

I'm working on the building;
It's a sure foundation;
I'm holding up the bloodstained banner for my Lord.
Just as soon as I get through working on the building,
I'm going up to Heaven, to get my reward.

She faithfully worked on all twelve of our buildings, and then, at the age of sixty-two, she concluded, like the apostle Paul before her:

I have fought a good fight, I have finished my course, I have kept the faith.   2 Timothy 4:7

It was June of 1970 when Mama declared that she was *"ready to be offered up,"* for *"the time of [her] departure was at hand"* (2 Timothy 4:6). Then she boarded that Glory Train, smiled, waved at all of us, and left us in the hands of the Lord.

Our sweet Mama, whom we all had depended on so much, was gone from this world, but she left us something precious, a memory. She will forever be cherished in our hearts.

TRIED IN THE FIRE

Oh, children, love and obey your parents. You only have one opportunity to do it—while they're still in this world. Don't risk waking up one day and realizing their value to you, only to discover that it's too late.

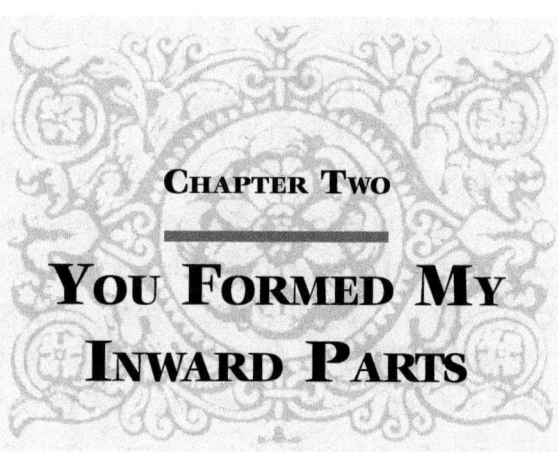

Chapter Two

You Formed My Inward Parts

For You formed my inward parts;
You wove me in my mother's womb.
I will give thanks to You, for I am fearfully and wonderfully made;
Wonderful are Your works,
And my soul knows it very well.
My frame was not hidden from You,
When I was made in secret,
And skillfully wrought in the depths of the earth;
Your eyes have seen my unformed substance;
And in Your book were all written
The days that were ordained for me,
When as yet there was not one of them.

          Psalm 139:13-16, NAS

Because I was born in October, I started school a month before my birthday. As far back as I can remember, I was a very unusual child. I was always getting into things, and calamity seemed to follow me everywhere I went.

Infected with Ringworm

That first year, my teacher was Miss Edwinor Porter, a pretty young woman, who always called for a short rest period each morning and, again, each afternoon. During these times, we would lay our heads on the desk and take a short nap. There was nothing wrong with that, but I never have figured out to this day why she sat a certain boy next to me (at the same desk). As I remember it, there were enough desks to go around, so it didn't seem to make sense for us to be seated together.

I had a lovely head of hair, but when my head touched his, I contracted ringworm, a dreadful fungus infection that usually caused all your hair to fall out. I remember the pungent smell of the Glovers Mange, mixed with hair grease, that my older sister Fedie used to treat my scalp. My hair never grew back as beautiful as it had once been, but thank God for perms and straightening combs.

Burned by Fire

Several years later, I was looking into our potbellied room heater one day, to see why it wasn't heating very well. We burned both wood and coal in it. I poured some kerosene into the fire, to see if I could make it heat up faster, and when the air hit the fumes from that kerosene, flames gushed out and burned most of my face.

YOU FORMED MY INWARD PARTS

Mama was worried that the flame had gotten down my windpipe. We had heard about children dying when that happened. She prayed, and the Lord preserved me, according to the promise of Isaiah:

> *I have called thee by thy name; thou art mine. When thou passest through the waters, I will be with thee; and through the rivers, they shall not overflow thee: when thou walkest through the fire, thou shalt not be burned; neither shall the flame kindle upon thee.* Isaiah 43:1-2

> ***My burns did not become infected, and Fedie was there to nurse them faithfully!***

This was a literal trial by fire, and over the coming days, God's protective power was with me. My burns did not become infected, and Fedie was there to nurse them faithfully. Thankfully, there was no permanent scaring.

Fedie was enough older than me that she became like another mother. That's why I still to this day call her my sister/mother, or my sister/mama. She was to play a major role in my future.

TRIED IN THE FIRE

BURNED AGAIN

A few years later, Daddy converted all of our wood and coal stoves to oil. He kept the oil container to fill them under the kitchen table. One day I was checking to make sure there was enough oil in the can, and was innocently using a match to help me see the fluid level. The fumes from the oil caught fire and exploded in my face. There was a loud boom, and fire gushed out and burned me a second time.

Looking down the spout of an oil container with a match was not a very smart thing to do. About that time, I began to understand that the enemy was bent on killing me or leaving me permanently scarred for life. He knew that one day I would become an instrument in the hands of the Master Potter, and, therefore, he sought to wreak havoc on my young life.

That's a lesson we can all learn. The enemy will try to hurt you or kill you, but whatever you do, don't give in to him. Hold on to God's unchanging hand, and stand on His Word. Satan is determined to stand against God's master plan for our lives. In my case, I was again spared because of the prayers of my parents, and there was no permanent scaring.

BEATEN IN SCHOOL

When I was in the fifth grade, my teacher, Mrs. Branch, put me across the umbrella stand in the cloakroom one day and beat me with a stick, because I was late getting to school. The school, Hyde Park Elementary, was about a

YOU FORMED MY INWARD PARTS

mile from our house, and we had to walk to get there. That mile sometimes seemed like three or four miles to us.

After that, I would walk awhile and then run awhile, and all the time I was crying, wondering if I could make it in the school door before the tardy bell rang. That day, I hadn't been able to make it, and I had to suffer the consequences.

Looking back on that experience now, I realize that beating is one of the processes used to refine gold.

He made the candlestick of pure gold: of beaten work made he the candlestick. Exodus 37:17

At the time, however, I wasn't very happy about what Mrs. Branch had done to me. She also had to face the wrath of my sister Sarah and her friend Bessie Mae. What they said to her that day seemed to be effective, for she never beat me again after that. There should have been a law against such child abuse, but when I look back, I realize that it was good for me. A little discipline never hurt anyone.

In those days, we could never have used the excuse that we had a "short attention span." The fear of punishment created in us a seriousness about our work. There were no interruptions in *our* class, and the teachers were able to do what they do best—teach. We came out of that school experience excelling in reading, writing, and arithmetic.

TRIED IN THE FIRE

THE BRIGHTER SIDE OF MY SCHOOL EXPERIENCE

For a time, it seemed that I was on a smoother path and was not suffering any new calamities. I continued with my elementary school education and loved every moment of it.

I sang soprano in the Glee Club, and once a year we "colored folk," as everyone called us in those days, held our May Day Festival at the big City Auditorium downtown. It was a festive occasion, and each year we opened with *Welcome, Sweet Springtime, We Bring You this Song*. This festival always occurred just before graduation.

In each of our local schools, we celebrated May Day by wrapping the May Pole, and that was another colorful event. I wonder if this current generation is still doing things like that. The next time I visit a school, I must inquire.

The May Day celebrations represented a time when we could dress in pretty white (and also colorful) dresses. In that day, all girls wore dresses, and all boys wore

> *For a time, it seemed that I was on a smoother path and was not suffering any new calamities!*

pants. That's not to say they were always new. Daddy and Mama could only afford new clothes and shoes for us on certain occasions. Some of those were: the beginning of school, Christmas, Easter, May Day, prom, and graduation.

The elementary school year was now nearing its end. By early June, it would all be over. May, therefore, was a month for special activities, tests, and spring concerts.

Our music teacher, Mrs. Lundy, would take us every year to a little subdivision of Memphis called Orange Mound, where we would sing in her church. Those were happy moments that we never forgot. Our joy over these trips wasn't nearly as much about going outside the school to sing as it was visiting the ice cream factory (Kinkle Brother's) not far from Mrs. Lundy's church. There they had the best dixie cups, with three flavors (vanilla, chocolate, and strawberry). They always gave us a little wooden spoon to eat it with, and I loved scraping that ice cream ever so slowly, so that it would last for as long as possible. That was fun, because money was scarce in those days, and treats were not available very often.

FUN CHOPPING COTTON AND SHELLING PEAS

I was very adventurous, so one day I asked my mother if I could go with some of my friends and their chaperons to chop cotton. There were no cotton fields near where we lived, but a truck would come by and pick us up before daybreak to take us over into Arkansas. When my friends had told me what fun they had on the truck and how they had taken the few pennies they earned picking cotton and bought bologna, souse, cheese, and crackers, I was excited. That sounded like quite an adventure.

Mama let me go, and I remember chopping cotton in the hot sun. I was having a wonderful time ... until the man in charge of the field came over to me and ordered me back to the truck. He said that I was chopping down his cotton plants instead of the weeds.

I was embarrassed by that, but later I asked Mama if I could go again, this time to pick cotton. I thought I might do better at picking than at chopping, and, sure enough, I did. It was an all-day trip, and I don't think they paid us more than twenty-five cents (fifty, at the most). But even that was a lot of money for a young girl in those days. I loved picking cotton in the hot sun and having fun with other young people.

I recall going down the street sometimes to Mr. Tate's house to shell peas and beans. We sat on the porch for hours, laughing, teasing, and shelling. He would measure them out and give us a penny a pint. I suppose he might have taken advantage of us sometimes, because we were so young, but we had fun working with the other children anyway.

Off to New York for the Summer

In 1948, I graduated from the eighth grade, and Fedie, who was now married and living in New York, sent for me to come and keep her daughter (my niece) Esther, while she worked. I remember riding that beautiful train

YOU FORMED MY INWARD PARTS

(the Tennessean), and having to change trains in Washington, D.C. The train passed one spot where we could catch a glimpse of the White House. How exciting that was!

To go on to New York, I had to change to the Pennsylvanian, a much older train, but since it would take only five or six hours to reach Penn Station in New York, that was fine with me.

In those days, they had very limited seating on trains for blacks, and the rest of the train was reserved for whites only. In the dining car, they had one little table for blacks. It was clearly marked by a sign that read: Coloreds Only. I suppose the limited seating and eating arrangements for blacks was because most black families couldn't afford to ride trains much in those days. Anyway, we knew, for sure, where our place was. Thank God for Rosa Parks and Martin Luther King, Jr., who suffered and gave themselves to break down the walls of prejudice.

I arrived in New York safely, because Mama was praying, and God sent His angels to protect me as I traveled. I remember how excited I was when I saw my big sister, Mama Fedie. I knew then that all would be well. My real Mama trusted Fedie implicitly, and that's why she let me go to New York for the summer.

EXPLORING THE BIG APPLE

In New York, I had to find things to do during the day, while Fedie was at work. Every day Esther and I would go out and explore. We liked to go to Gertz Department

Store, where we would ride up and down the escalator. Sometimes we would take a bus and go over the Whitestone Bridge, just to view the beautiful scenery. Then we would come back on the next bus. We enjoyed our explorations and tried to always be home before Fedie came home from work.

One day we took a walk to Forty School Playground in Jamaica. Esther loved the outdoors, and she was enjoying swinging and going down the slide. Then, suddenly a gang of young boys approached us and began to yell at us to get out of the park. I refused, and they jumped on me and beat me up. I was left bleeding, crying, swollen, wounded, and very sad. They might have killed me, but God didn't let them do it.

When I got home and everyone found out what had happened, Fedie and her husband went out hunting those boys. Fortunately, they were not able to find them.

As the boys had been beating me, they were also making fun of my southern accent. That made me determined to change the way I talked. Within days, I had adopted many of the northern characteristics of speech. You do what you have to, and it's called survival. God had kept me safe yet again.

That summer, Fedie bought me some of the prettiest dresses and a pair of lovely black patent leather shoes that I never forgot. I had my picture taken in New York in my new clothes, and when I went back home, I was now one of the sharpest dressers in high school.

Chapter Three
I Put Away Childish Things

When I was a child, I spake as a child, I understood as a child, I thought as a child: but when I became a man, I put away childish things.   1 Corinthians 13:11

When I started attending Manassas High School, I had to ride two buses to get there. I don't recall them having school passes in those days, but I'll never forget us having to sit at the back of the bus. When we got closer to our school, we had the whole bus to ourselves. We survived, because it was a way of life.

Amazingly, one of the things I remember most about high school is our chapel services and how God was given a place in our school day. Our assistant principal, Mr. Teague, often read to us from 1 Corinthians 13. He especially loved that eleventh verse. I'm sure he wanted us to grow up and become men and women.

TRIED IN THE FIRE

How sad that prayer and Bible reading have been taken out of our schools! The replacements seem to be weapons, drugs, and the disruption of the classroom. All of that was unheard of in my day. We knew how to behave. After all, they still believed in using thick leather straps as a means of discipline.

> *How sad that prayer and Bible reading have been taken out of our schools!*

THAT WIDE LEATHER STRAP

Having an overall grade average below a C was cause for a whipping. I made that mistake only once. We were lined up on stage in front of the entire student body, and our hands were smacked with that wide leather strap. I never got another D, because I didn't want to suffer the shame and embarrassment of having the other students sit there and laugh at me. It wasn't funny.

WANTING TO "HANG OUT" WITH FRIENDS

When I began wanting to "hang out" with my friends, I came up against Mama's strict sense of right and wrong. She rarely allowed us to do that. There were so many of us that we had enough chores to keep us busy at home anyway, and we kept each other company.

I PUT AWAY CHILDISH THINGS

Sometimes, though, I was allowed to visit my friends Norma Jean and Vera Black, who lived at the corner of our street and Hollywood. Those were rare occasions, but sometimes Mama did give in.

We had another friend, Viola, who lived not too far away on Hollywood Street. These girls were from respectable families, and their parents were also strict and taught them well. Mama didn't object to *that* kind of friendship. But it could be misleading and dangerous.

One day, these three girls asked if I could go with them downtown. Mama let me go, not realizing their intent—to take a closer look at the handsome guys we had all heard worked at the Peabody Hotel.

We timed our trip wisely, knowing that the hotel had inspection every morning about 11:00 AM. Those handsome young black men would be lined up for us to look over. Some of them were light skinned with nice hair, and some were brown skinned with nice hair. Every boy had his hair groomed, so even if it wasn't exceptional, it looked good to us.

We waited for the inspection to be completed, and then we talked with some of the boys. They liked what they saw and asked if they could take us out in the next few days. We were delighted.

Our adventure was not yet over. While we were down there, we just had to go by the Harlem House and get one of their juicy "dogs" before returning home. These were hot dogs, deep fried in grease, and then topped with chili sauce and ketchup. Oh, my! That was good eating!

TRIED IN THE FIRE

Mama's Wisdom

When I got home, I asked Mama if I could go with the other three girls on a quadruple date. "No, Gwen," she said. "I don't feel comfortable letting you go with them." I was quite disappointed and probably pouted (as they called it in those days), but I wouldn't let Mama see me do it. Her word was law in our house, and I didn't want to get a slap across my mouth. If she had seen me pouting, she would have told me to "pull that lip in," so I just grinned—while she was watching. Young people didn't express themselves nearly as much in those days. They were "seen and not heard."

A few months later, all three of my friends seemed to blossom in their stomach area. To everyone's amazement, they were all three pregnant. Two of the guys married two of the girls, but my friend Norma Jean's date didn't marry her. When all of this happened, I was so glad that I had listened to Mama.

Young people, it pays to have a concerned mother who hears from God. Learn to trust and obey her instincts. Young people everywhere should always listen to their moms, especially if they're saved. Even if they're not, the Bible teaches us to honor our parents, and it gives us a promise for doing so:

Children, obey your parents in the Lord: for this is right. Honour thy father and mother; which is the first commandment with promise; that it may be well with thee, and thou mayest live long on the earth.

Ephesians 6:1-3

I PUT AWAY CHILDISH THINGS

Would you like to live a long time? Then know that godly parents seem to have an express line to Heaven, and because of their love for you, the Lord shares little secrets with them. They know your thoughts afar off, because He knows them. They seem to know the end from the beginning, because He knows it.

Watch who you keep company with. Mama often told us that one bad apple could spoil the whole barrel, and it's true.

OUR FAVORITE PASTIME

Our parents didn't allow us to do what we wanted to in the home either. They lived by the Word of God. One of their favorite verses was this:

> *But as for me and my house, we will serve the LORD.*
> Joshua 24:15

In our house, we spent our days, as children, playing church. We imitated the saints: preaching, dancing, prophesying, and speaking in tongues. We thought it was great fun.

We could imitate the way most of the saints talked and acted, and each of us had our favorites to imitate. How we loved to imitate Mother Lillie Mae Thomas and the way she danced in the Spirit and walked in the gift of prophecy. She was always right on time with the messages God gave her, and that made us fear the Lord in her. She was the type of person whom we could pattern our lives after.

TRIED IN THE FIRE

Sister Thomas is still alive today and still sharp at ninety-two. She still leads the early Sunday morning prayer meeting at one of the local churches, counsels, prophesies, and encourages me and many others of God's people. What a wonderful testimony!

GOING TO CHURCH

We had to go to church during the week and all day on Sunday, and we were always on time for Sunday school and morning worship. Every Saturday night, Mama cooked, and we ironed, had our hair done, and were sure that we would be ready for church the next day.

There was another reason we did it on Saturday night. Among other things, we were not allowed to set up the ironing board on Sunday. No department stores and no grocery stores were open that day. If we forgot something or we needed something, that was just too bad. We had to do without. Sunday was our Sabbath, a day set aside to honor God.

On Sunday evening, we went back to church for YPWW (Young People's Willing Workers), our youth meeting, and the evening worship service. We also attended any and all revivals that were scheduled. I wonder now how we were able to become honor students in school, considering all the activities our parents had us participate in. Only God knows, but we did it.

WE WERE MISCHIEVOUS

Like normal children everywhere, we were mischievous when we could get away with it. For instance,

I PUT AWAY CHILDISH THINGS

sometimes, when Mama had gone out for a little while, we turned on a secular radio station that played the blues. One of our favorite singers was B.B. King. One of us would keep an eye out the front door to see when Mama was coming. When we saw her crossing the bridge on our street, we would run through the house, trying to finish up our chores and quickly change the radio back to a Gospel station.

Like children, we were typically active, often a little bad, and occasionally disobedient, even though we knew we had been taught better. Many times, for instance, I didn't finish my assigned chore of washing the dishes. Instead, I paid the twins to do it. Sometimes, however, they would go out to buy candy with the pennies I had paid them and leave the dishes still undone. Then, when Mama got home, I was punished for it. That infuriated me. I had paid them to do that work, and they hadn't done it. They were in trouble with me ... temporarily at least. I always forgave them and trusted them again, after a few days.

> *Like children, we were typically active, often a little bad, and occasionally disobedient!*

TRIED IN THE FIRE

A Near-Death Experience

One day, I went to the swimming pool in Orange Mound without telling anyone where I was going. I couldn't swim at all, and, instead of wading in the shallow water, I decided to go into the deep section (it was ten feet deep). I held onto a rope for support, but the rope was not intended for that purpose; it was only a divider. When I finally lost my balance and began to fall into the water, I didn't even know enough to hold my nose.

At that point, I was too embarrassed to call for help from the lifeguard, sitting up on his stand. I could never imagine why he didn't see me floundering in the water, but he didn't. And, so, for a few moments, my life hung in the balance.

When I think of how Peter, who began to sink as he was trying to walk on water, called out to the Lord to save him, I'm not sure why I was too embarrassed to cry for help.

The lifeguard may not have seen my dilemma that day, but there was One who did. He is not only our Savior, but He is also our Friend. His Word declares:

And it shall come to pass, that before they call, I will answer; and while they are yet speaking, I will hear.
Isaiah 65:24

And that's exactly what God did for me that day. Just when I thought my life had ended, I was suddenly able to grab hold of the side of the pool and pull myself out. God has planned our lives, and He will not let the devil destroy us—when we are guarded by prayer power.

I knew that I should have asked Mama's permission before I left home that day, and I should have let her know where I was going. I didn't deserve God's help, but He helped me anyway.

Young people, always let someone know where you're going. That's a form of protection for your own life. Be accountable to someone. I could have drowned that day, but thank God He kept me—even during the years before I totally surrendered my life to Him.

The Prom

It was almost the end of my high school years, and it was prom season. My sister Sarah bought me a beautiful dress, and I went to the prom with a handsome young boy from Hamilton High School (for some reason, they seemed to have the most handsome fellows at that school). I'd never gone out with a boy before, and I was very green. After the prom, we didn't go drinking, getting high on drugs, or having sex (as some young people do these days). Instead, we had a lot of clean fun. Mama knew we would, and that's why she let us go.

We just socialized, ate, talked, went to the park, and sat on a bench until early in the morning. We didn't reserve hotel rooms, so that we could brag about having sexual encounters and how much fun it was. I remembered my upbringing and was afraid to do the wrong things, for fear that I would bring shame upon myself and my family. Even though I was in the twelfth grade and close to my graduation day, I was still under my parent's roof, and I wanted them to be proud of me.

Mama was looking out for me. She didn't go to sleep until I was home safely that night. That's what a caring mother does.

> *I was still under my parent's roof, and I wanted them to be proud of me!*

My High School Graduation

Graduation night finally arrived. This was my big night! Our high school always held its graduation at the big Memphis City Auditorium. That night, the city buses went on strike. What a tragedy! We all wanted to "hang out," but the public transportation had shut down, and we had no way of getting around. This was outrageous; we had to find a way around this situation.

Well, who needed the public buses anyway? we decided. We would just get a ride with someone—something we should have known better than to do and for which we were sure to be sorry. We ended up at a bar and grill

I PUT AWAY CHILDISH THINGS

called Sarah's & Arah's, and my friends started looking around for some airmen stationed at nearby Millington Air Force Base. They didn't find what they were looking for, so we went on to Beulah's Tavern. There I met two young Army brothers: Staff Sergeant William Stafford and his brother, Master Sergeant Charles Stafford.

"What are you doing down here with those girls?" they asked me. "You don't belong here."

When I didn't agree with them immediately, they insisted, "Come on, let's get our car. We're taking you home."

I was only too happy to oblige, again, something I knew I should not be doing. I could have gotten into serious trouble that night ... if the prayers of my mother had not been following me closely.

All I can say is that the Lord was with me. The girls I was with were not wholesome girls, and I could very easily have gotten involved with something that night that I would have regretted for the rest of my life. The men knew the girls I was with and knew what kind of reputation they had. Still, out of the clear blue, they chose to take me home. They could tell that I was innocent. What a miracle! There seems to be a mark upon the children of the saints.

First Impressions

The staff sergeant was driving a Rocket 88 Oldsmobile, and right away I thought that he was my kind of man—light skinned with pretty hair. (There I went again, judging a man by his looks, rather than by his character.) But even though I was attracted to the younger man, it seemed to be the older one who was interested in me.

I was due to leave soon for New York again, to stay with Fedie and begin some type of career. I already had my train ticket and the date of my departure. God's master plan was in place, and I had no business getting involved with an older man, an Air Force man, who just might have a wife and children back home waiting for him.

I would like to speak very clearly to the young ladies reading this book. Please don't be so hard up for a pair of pants that you'll drop your guard and let any man (or piece of a man) destroy your life. Young men, you have to watch yourselves too. In my day, it was the men who pursued the women. Now, women are openly pursuing men. They not only invite men out on dates; they propose to them. Believe me, you don't want that. The Lord said in His Word:

> *Whoso findeth a wife findeth a good thing, and obtaineth favour of the* L<small>ORD</small>.   Proverbs 18:22

Let that loose woman go, for God has someone better for you.

O<small>FF TO</small> N<small>EW</small> Y<small>ORK</small> A<small>GAIN</small>

When we got to our house that night, my mother was very impressed with these young men's respectful attitude toward both me and her. A few days later, that

I PUT AWAY CHILDISH THINGS

master sergeant drove me to the train station (with Mama's permission). He got on the train to help me get settled into my seat, and he put all of my things into the overhead baggage compartment. Shortly afterward, we heard the conductor saying, "All Aboard!" and knew that it was time to part.

I walked him to the door, so that he could get off the train, but before stepping down, he took me in his arms and kissed me. It was a kiss I never forgot. Thank God he hadn't done that days before. It was very good timing, because kisses like that have a way of making your toes tingle. Thank God for His keeping power. I was safely on my way to New York.

CHAPTER FOUR
TO GIVE YOU AN EXPECTED END

For I know the thoughts that I think toward you, saith the LORD, *thoughts of peace, and not of evil, to give you an expected end.*   Jeremiah 29:11

I arrived in New York on that beautiful train, the Tennessean, and Fedie once again met me. She took me to an apartment building where, she said, she was living temporarily. She and her husband had separated, and she had to live somewhere else while he got all of this things moved out of their apartment at the Alfred E. Smith Housing Projects. The temporary place was in Harlem, but she assured me that it would only be for a few days.

LIVING TEMPORARILY IN THE SLUMS OF HARLEM

When we got to the place, I could see why she had warned me. It was an unbelievable sight. People threw their trash out the windows, and that's what I had to wake up to every morning. I surely didn't want to live there any longer than necessary.

I Met a Man

I spent some time walking on the streets in Harlem during the day, and there I met a young man working in a florist shop. He was a handsome guy, and he asked to take me out. I didn't know what Mama Fedie would think of this.

As it turned out, my sister said that I *could* go out once in a while—if she felt comfortable with the young man who had invited me, but I would have to be home before dark. This young man passed her test. Our dates consisted of going out to have a hamburger and some fries, going to the park, sitting and chatting a while, and then coming home to talk about what a great time we'd had.

I liked the guy a lot, and, knowing that I would soon be moving out of Harlem back to Fedie's apartment, I got up my nerve and told him that I was pregnant, hoping to hold on to him for a while. We had never had sex, but because we were not trained in sex education in those days, I thought you could get pregnant from simply hugging and kissing. My ploy didn't work. He knew more about sex than I did, and I never saw him again.

An Empty Apartment Is Transformed

We moved back to Fedie's apartment, but it was empty. Her husband had taken everything. When I went out one

TO GIVE YOU AN EXPECTED END

day, the place was looking rather barren and dismal, but when I came back later, it was full of beautiful furniture, and everything was nicely arranged. I smelled some good beans and corn bread cooking on the stove.

Mama Fedie was a wonderful cook, an exquisite housekeeper, a very professional worker, and a sharp dresser to boot. And she taught me to excel at all those things.

DANCING THE CALYPSO

Fedie knew many families in the projects, and one woman, in particular, was her friend. We called her Little Julia.

Little Julia had a brother who was rather ugly, but when he asked me to go dancing with him at Hunt's Point Palace, I agreed to go. I'd never danced before, so when we got out on the dance floor, I just started shaking my hips like everyone else. They called the dance they were doing the calypso.

> *They called the dance they were doing the calypso!*

Then, before I knew what was happening, everyone had cleared the floor except the two of us. They had all formed a ring around us, and they were applauding like I knew what I was doing. I didn't.

Where that ability to dance came from I never knew. I'd never done the calypso in my life. I was learning that

Satan can make us professionals at things we've never dreamed possible. I knew that, instead of being out on some dance floor, I should have been in church, worshipping the Lord, but because we had been brought up so strict, I felt that I wanted to experience life in the world.

Why did I do that? It was just a trick of the enemy. I should have known better, but, like so many others, I was deceived. Still, the Father would not allow the enemy to destroy me, even though I was playing on the edge of the precipice.

When you get loose from godly ties and choose to go the devil's way, life can become *"hard."* Solomon wrote:

> *Good understanding giveth favour; but the way of the transgressors is hard.* Proverbs 13:15

Nevertheless, Christian mothers need to stop worrying so much about their child. Instead, they should give them space and trust God to keep them. We have an expression that says: "give him enough rope, and he'll hang himself." That's true enough, but always remember what happened with the prodigal son. He eventually came back home, and in the process, he learned his lesson.

MY FIRST JOB

I found a job pulling television parts out of a barrel, but a problem arose very quickly. The boss was attracted to me and kept making passes at me, asking me out. I refused. I knew he was married, and I'd been taught by

TO GIVE YOU AN EXPECTED END

Mama to *"abstain from [even] the appearance of evil"* (1 Thessalonians 5:22). I refused to lose my virtue to any man, even this one who was handsome, Jewish, and prestigious. After all, he owned the business. I dared not yield to his persistent advances, for I couldn't afford to "mess up" my life. I wasn't yet saved, but I *was* concerned about what Mama would think.

ANOTHER FACTORY JOB

When the boss' conduct didn't improve, I decided to change jobs. I found another job at Emsig Button Factory in New York City. It was much further away from where I lived, but otherwise it seemed to be ideal. It was not, by any stretch of the imagination, a good job. Now, instead of scooping television parts out of barrels, I was scooping buttons.

I was forced to work in factories in those early days because I hadn't taken any business courses in high school. Our classes were scheduled according to future ambitions, and mine had been to become a teacher. Therefore, I was given a general education program, and it didn't include typing, shorthand, and other skills that would have come in handy about then.

While dipping buttons out of those barrels, I kept desiring a better job, but I didn't know how to go about getting one. The Lord knew.

One day, I arrived at the plant, and it was ice cold in there. I said to the girls I was working with, "I'm not working in here. It's too cold. The Health Department would shut this place down if they knew it was this cold in here." I told them I was going into the lounge and wait until the boss came. Another employee walked out behind me, and most of the other ladies followed.

When the boss came in, he asked, "Who started this?"

They all answered, "Gwen Gandy."

The man began laying everybody off, one by one, until he got to me, and he laid me off too. A few days later, he called the others back to work, but I was left without a job. He had mistakenly thought that I was a troublemaker.

> *He called the others back to work, but I was left without a job!*

Yet Another Dead-end Job

The local union placed me on another job, this one in a shoe binding factory. The lady next to me would unwind shoe binding from a spool, and then I would guide it into a barrel. It was an easy job, but not one that promised much of a future. I guess I could say that I was the "Chief Spooler" at that plant, but that wasn't saying much.

I heard that the New York Telephone Company was hiring and decided to go there and apply. I passed the

TO GIVE YOU AN EXPECTED END

test, and then waited, hoping to be called. I had been on my latest dead-end job for several months now, and I desperately wanted to find something better.

When I still didn't get a call, my desperation increased. Was there no way out of this job? I called Mama and asked her to pray that God would give me the other job soon. I'm sure that she must have prayed. When she asked God for anything that was His will, something always happened.

One day my boss kept staring at me … until it became so obvious and so annoying that I began to stare back at him. "What are you staring at?" he asked.

"At you," I answered.

"Well, you're fired," he said.

"Then give me my check," I answered.

"Come back on Friday."

"No," I insisted. "You fired me today, so give me my check today. If not, I'll go outside and get a 'cop,' and he'll make you pay me." You could do that in those days.

I'm sure this man must have been thinking to himself, "This woman's crazy. Let me get her out of here." Whatever he was thinking, he told the secretary to write me a check as quickly as possible. She did, and I was happy to be out of there.

I sensed that I was now headed to the destiny God had waiting for me. I wasn't sure what had happened; the boss and I had gotten along fine until that day. But God knows how to move us on when it's His time.

Finding My Place

Thinking about it later, I realized what had happened. The telephone company had called the plant, asking for references. It seems to me that this was against the law at the time, but it happened anyway. That explained why my boss was suddenly angry and wanting to fire me, before I had a chance to quit.

When I realized this, I went to the phone and called the telephone company immediately. "Someone from your office called my place of employment, asking for references, and it caused me to lose my job," I told them. "Now, if you don't hire me, I'll go to the NAACP, the Amsterdam News, and anybody else I can think of and cry out against this injustice." That tone seemed to have the desired effect.

In those days, every large company had a certain quota of blacks they had to hire, and maybe hiring me would have pushed the phone company over its quota. But I didn't care; I just needed a decent job. Probably, I reasoned, they didn't have many blacks at all.

I was accepted, I passed my physical exam, and I was on the job within two weeks.

One Other Black

It was just as I had thought. There was only one other black, a young high yellow lady, working in the AMA (Automated Message Accounting) office of the phone company. Her name was June Graves. June and I became good friends and worked as a team.

TO GIVE YOU AN EXPECTED END

There were a lot of special activities within the company. They had group meetings for the Red Cross, the Blood Drive, the United Way, and many other charities. The company believed in supporting these agencies with their time, their money, and their employees.

UNHEALTHY ASPECTS OF THE COMPANY

During our regular pep meetings, the company served coffee, tea, and Danish, but they also had various brands of cigarettes free for anyone who wanted to smoke them. This was all arrayed on the conference tables. We all took advantage of the freebies, and I'm sure that many became hooked on nicotine for life in this way. I was fortunate. I tried to smoke occasionally, just to be cool, but it never appealed to me much.

The company also had Christmas parties, where members of management and the employees had the opportunity to start ungodly relationships. This resulted in many unearned promotions.

I WOULD HAVE TO BE ONE OF THE BEST

I knew that I had to be one of the best on the job in order to make a statement to the company. I didn't want them to ever be sorry they had hired me. Because of that, I was a stickler for getting to work on time, and I didn't miss a single day in two years. Even if I was sick, I never stayed home. Instead, I went to work and then let them send me to Medical (and they sent me home). I worked hard and excelled at every responsibility. It also didn't hurt that Mama's prayers were with me.

Working for the Union

In time, I was chosen to be Chairlady for the entire downstate telephone company union. As Chairlady, I had ten representatives under my supervision, and between us, we covered the entire Eastern Region. We were a fair labor union that fought for justice for our members and helped those who had been overlooked for promotion to be reconsidered. In most cases, we were successful.

In my capacity as Chairlady, I worked with a tough Irish woman by the name of Mildred Dennen. Mildred had platinum blond hair that she wore short, and the prettiest blue eyes, but she was all business. When she said something, she was serious about it.

The big bosses were afraid of Mildred. She had taken Management to court, causing many vice presidents to be removed from their positions in the process. She was not a person to be toyed with.

In 1955, my hourly wage was the princely sum of $15.00 an hour, when I was on union business. That was big money in those days. The union position opened many doors of opportunity to me. I didn't know it, but I was in training for the greater things to come.

An Orphan Tugged at My Heartstrings

I headed an investigation by the company into the various agencies that made up the United Way. Large amounts of money were being set aside for such work, and the company wanted to know that their funds were well spent.

I'll never forget the day I went to a children's day care center, sponsored by United Way, and an adorable three-year-old boy ran and jumped into my arms. I seemed to have always had a way with boys (large and small), but everybody was amazed at how this little fellow took to me. His teacher told us that both of his parents were blind and, thus, had never set eyes upon their darling child. He stole my heart, and, as I was leaving that day, I found myself longing to pack him up and take him home with me. At the time, that was impossible. But I did let the telephone company know that the orphanage was an agency worthy of their sponsorship.

> *We were a fair labor union that fought for justice for our members!*

BLESSED WITH HIGH-PAYING POSITIONS

With less than two years on the job, I had been chosen to represent thousands of employees at the telephone company. This was nothing but the favor of God. Then, after two years of service with the company, I was promoted to a grade-five position. This gave me an opportunity to learn other jobs, especially with data machines. From that time on, I was blessed with high paying positions. My IQ, I was told, was comparable to that of a college graduate, and I hadn't yet done any college-level training. I did have God's promise:

Wisdom and might are his.   Daniel 2:20

To God be all the glory!

Mildred Dennen also received a promotion, and was now one of the company vice presidents. I wondered if they were thinking, "If you can't beat them, join them." Whatever the case, this fine lady was moving on up.

Preparation for Greater Things

God is a good God, and He has good things in store for each of us. He's just waiting for us to be willing to honor and serve Him. Jesus said:

For many are called, but few are chosen.
                                              Matthew 22:14

When we *are* chosen, we will experience stiff opposition, so we must be well prepared. God is calling His children to be a force against evil in this world, and He needs us to be well trained. Often, it is a secular opportunity that gives us the type of training we need. Once we have the necessary training, God will promote us. In the meantime, be sweet, and be the best employee in the company. Your day of promotion is coming.

In my position with the phone company and the union, I was always available for special projects, and I helped out wherever I could—even training others. I was not like some who believe that it is best to keep everything to themselves, thinking that this guarantees them job security. I was always giving out, believing for God to give me more. And He always did.

CHAPTER FIVE
I WILL BLESS THEE

*Now the L*ORD *had said unto Abram, Get thee out of thy country, and from thy kindred, and from thy father's house, unto a land that I will shew thee: and I will make of thee a great nation, and I will bless thee, and make thy name great; and thou shalt be a blessing: and I will bless them that bless thee, and curse him that curseth thee: and in thee shall all families of the earth be blessed.* Genesis 12:1-3

Mama Fedie and her husband reconciled, and I had to pack my things and prepare to move. She helped me find a place of my own in Brooklyn.

MY OWN PLACE

In those days, landlords rented out single rooms, and I found a very beautiful room. I would have to share the kitchen and bathrooms with several other ladies. In that way, I met Queenie Sheffield and Ollie Floyd. They were from Florida, and we became very good friends.

Our landlord was an older, single man, whom everyone called a "preacher," but while we were living in his house, we never saw him walking in that anointing. He was fresh, and he was funny. One night he told me, "If you get tired of playing Solitaire, I know a game that two can play."

I thought, "Why, you old rascal!" I told my friends what he had said, and we all decided to avoid him as much as possible in the future.

> *"If you get tired of playing Solitaire, I know a game that two can play!"*

A Severe Physical Test

During my stay in that house, I was overtaken with a sickness that I, at first, thought was just a cold or flu. When my temperature soared to 104.8, I was rushed to King's County Hospital.

The doctors at King's County immediately admitted me and set to work to try to bring the fever down. There were nurses stationed at the door of my ward on duty around the clock, and both doctors and interns began to take tests, poking and probing me, trying to find some logical cause for the high fever. After nearly three days of tests, they finally came to the conclusion that I had a rare form of rheumatic fever, usually only found in Asia, and they began to treat me the best they could.

But that wasn't saying much. There was little that could be done in those days for this sickness, and the doctors were not sure that I would ever fully recover.

Sarah and her husband had followed me to New York, and now I had a brother there too. My New York family visited me often in the hospital and told me not to worry. They also suggested that we not worry Mama with this sickness. They would take care of me, they said. But, because none of them was saved, I didn't feel comfortable with their suggestion. This was my life we were dealing with, and they seemed to have given up hope for me to have a normal future. They were saying things like they would see to that I got into a good nursing home. Can you imagine! I was just twenty-one, and they were making decisions like that about my future.

In Desperate Need of Prayer

At the time, our parents were the only ones who knew how to pray, and so I was determined to get a message to Mama. One day, when my brother-in-law William (now deceased), Sarah's husband, came to visit me (as he did every day on his lunch hour), I slipped him a letter that I'd written to Mama and asked him to send it

TRIED IN THE FIRE

Air Mail Special Delivery (today, we call it Express Mail). In those days, it cost about thirty-nine or forty cents to send a letter in this urgent way. That's the price of a regular postage stamp now. William mailed the letter, and I began to exercise my faith that it would accomplish its intended purpose.

My imagination went into overdrive that day. I could imagine them receiving that letter in the New York Post Office and putting it into a bag, that was then placed on a plane. The plane would land in Memphis, and the bag would be rushed to the Memphis Post Office. From there, the postman would get into his vehicle, drive to my mother's house, and knock on her door. I could imagine Mama answering, all excited because no one ever sent anything Special Delivery unless it was urgent. I could see her tearing open that envelope, reading my letter, then quickly calling other saints to ask them to join her in prayer. And, finally, I could envision my mother, as she set about to pray.

I knew she would first take time to call some other prayer warriors, because those saints always prayed as the Word of God teaches us:

Again I say unto you, That if two of you shall agree on earth as touching any thing that they shall ask, it shall be done for them of my Father which is in heaven. For where two or three are gathered together in my name, there am I in the midst of them.

Matthew 18:19-20

I WILL BLESS THEE

Today, more believers need to go back to this old-time way of prayer. It works.

I Was Healed

The very next time the nurses took my temperature, they were amazed to find that the fever had broken! As we sing in worship:

> *Glory be the Father,*
> *And to the Son,*
> *And to the Holy Ghost,*
> *As it was in the beginning*
> *Is now and ever shall be,*
> *World without end.*
> *Amen!*
> *Amen!*

God did a miracle for me that day, and it left the doctors baffled. They didn't know what had happened. About twelve of them gathered in my room, moving my bed to the middle of the floor, so that they could all gather around me.

"Gwendolyn," they asked, "what do you think was wrong with you? And why do you think it's now gone?"

I had not yet fully yielded my life to the Lord, and I was too embarrassed to tell them what I had done. My mother and other saints had prayed, and God had healed me. His Word declares:

TRIED IN THE FIRE

But he was wounded for our transgressions, he was bruised for our iniquities: the chastisement of our peace was upon him; and with his stripes we are healed.
Isaiah 53:5

Love had lifted me! As the grand old hymn of the church states:

I was sinking deep in sin,
Far from the peaceful shore,
Very deeply stained within,
Sinking to rise no more;
But the Master of the sea
Heard my despairing cry,
And from the water lifted me
Now safe am I.

In my case, "the water" had been my sickness. Just like that, God snatched me from the hand of death and from an early grave, and He made me whole. I was embarrassed to tell my doctors about it then, but no more. Now, I'll shout it from the housetops.

PRACTICING SEXUAL ABSTINENCE

I had several lady friends who believed in sexual abstinence, and we traveled together as much as possible. We never dated alone, only in couples. There were four of us who stuck together like glue: Sylvia (who drove a Thunderbird), Willie Mae, Judy, and myself. We all did the same thing. When a man would start to get overheated and ask WHEN, we would answer, "When we get married. That's when!"

We were determined to remain virtuous until Mr. Right came along. We were not only determined to be different; we were also determined to make a difference in the lives of the people around us.

I pray for young people today that they may be men and women of integrity. Young people, I urge you to keep your mind off of trashy things and to think clean thoughts. In the days ahead, I would be tested, and I would have to fight (literally sometimes) to keep from being taken advantage of, but I was determined.

> *God snatched me from the hand of death and from an early grave!*

Let me give you one example: I met a young lady name Mary who lived in Canarsie, and we seemed to hit it off. Together, we decided to go on a retreat in upstate New York. Her identical thirteen-year-old twin nephews went along. We were looking forward to having a very good time.

At the retreat center, there was swimming, row boating, and other outdoor sports available. I had always loved the outdoors, and was especially enamored of the beautiful nature trails in that place. One night, as we were walking along with a group, a man in the group began making a play for me. I wasn't attracted to him at all, but he pulled me close and tried to kiss me. That was a mistake.

When he did this, I took his arm, but then I twisted it behind his back and quickly brought him to his knees. He never tried that again.

"Are you sure you work for the telephone company," he said later, "or are you a lady wrestler?" My brothers had taught me well, and I wasn't about to let anyone take advantage of me.

Anxious to Get Married

Practicing abstinence for the time being was fine with me, but I *did* want to get married someday. And, as time passed and there were no suitable men on the horizon, I found myself becoming anxious about the matter, so anxious that I was about ready to say yes to any man who made me a proposal. I still had not yielded my life to the Lord, so it didn't occur to me to ask Him for a proper husband. Then I met Arthur.

Exactly where we met is lost in the recesses of time, but he seemed to be a very nice man, and he drove a brand new white Ford. I had always been attracted to guys with cars, and when they let *me* drive, as Arthur did, that was especially cool. Arthur and I hadn't known each other long before he said to me one night, "Gwen, let's get married."

I WILL BLESS THEE

I should have known enough not to respond immediately to such a proposal, but what came to my lips in that moment was just one word: "Okay!" And, with that, we started making wedding plans.

When we went to pick out rings, I learned that I would have to charge them on my credit. I had a good-paying job, and he was in the Army. That, alone, should have tipped me off to the fact that trouble lay ahead.

Oh, young ladies, never become so anxious to get married that you're willing to pay for everything. No man is worth all that. If he doesn't have the money needed to help pay for the initial expenses, then you'll probably be supporting him for the rest of your life. But all I could think about was: "I'm getting married!" I could now tell my colleagues that I, at last, had my man.

We talked to a preacher, reserved a hall, and I shopped for a gown. I was to have seven bridesmaids, a maid of honor, and a matron of honor. We all picked out our dresses, and they were hung in my closet. All we needed to do was to set a suitable date for the wedding.

I called Mama to ask her to pray about our upcoming marriage, and I let her speak with Arthur and also with his mother. I vaguely remember saying to Mama, "Pray that if it's God's will, everything will work out."

WHERE'S ARTHUR?

A few days before the wedding, I was trying to reach Arthur, and somehow I couldn't find him. I called his mother, but she couldn't tell me where he was. Then, I called his brothers, but nobody seemed to know his whereabouts. With just a day or so to go, I finally heard from Arthur. He had been picked up by MPs because he was AWOL. They had taken him to Fort Dix, New Jersey, and put him in the stockade. I canceled the wedding and caught a bus to Fort Dix, to visit my betrothed.

On the bus to Fort Dix, I met Thelma Dailey, a very attractive young lady, who was going to the same brig on the same base to visit a handsome young man, who looked like a young Wyatt Earp. He had a thick head of dark brown hair and a very nice complexion. After I got to know her, I asked if her husband might, perhaps, have a brother. No, he didn't have a brother, she told me, but he did have a good looking cousin. "Could you introduce me to him?" I asked. This shows just how madly in love with Arthur I was. As they say, "Out of sight, out of mind."

I did go to see Arthur several times, but his future didn't look very bright, and I wondered when, if ever, we might be able to finalize our marriage. Then the girl I had befriended on the bus invited me to spend the night at her apartment in the Bronx, and she called her husband's cousin to come over and meet me. His name was John L. Redd, and we were immediately attracted to each other. That was the end of Arthur. I never heard from him again.

JOHN L. REDD

John was a light skinned man, and the first time we dated, he came to pick me up, dressed in some khaki pants, a Tee shirt, and white bucks. He spoke with a strong southern accent, but I didn't mind that. He seemed to be the ideal man, and I believed that we could have beautiful children together. After all, wasn't that what marriage was all about?

We went to the movies that first time, and I had to pay. Again, that should have tipped me off, but I was slow to catch on. He was my dream man. We went out for about six months, and he never did take me anywhere expensive. For some reason, he never seemed to have any money. I should have known that something was wrong with that picture.

It wasn't long before John proposed, and, this time, I didn't call Mama and ask her to pray. I was afraid my dream man would disappear just as Arthur had. This time, I didn't even think about having a big wedding. I just wanted to be married to John. Surely we would live happily ever after—just like in the fairy tale books. I was getting "old." Twenty-five, in those days, was much too old for a girl not to be married and have children.

TRIED IN THE FIRE

Wedding Bells and My First Pregnancy

We were married in the living room of Pastor Chandler's house in Brooklyn. We had no place to stay, so we went to live with his sister Susie in her apartment on Koscuisko Street. It was located in the slums of Brooklyn, and for me, it was a nightmare. I was moving from a beautiful house to an apartment full of roaches and mice. Even though his sister kept the place clean, those apartments were infested, and I was accustomed to living in better-kept areas.

In no time at all, I was pregnant, and that was good news. At last, I could fulfill my dreams—having a baby. There was another reason I welcomed this moment. For years, I had suffered a lot with my menstrual cycles. Every month, seemingly on the same day, I had to be sent home from work with terrible cramps. This was the only thing that marred my perfect attendance record. I had been told that if I had a baby, all of that pain would end, and I desperately needed to make that happen.

Isn't that just like us humans, forever looking for easy ways out of our pain and misery? In doing this, we sometimes find relief, only to suffer other types of pain in the process.

The Meaning of Pregnancy

Today, young ladies think that they should get pregnant for a variety of reasons: Some think that it will cause their man to marry them. Some think they'll have a personal Barbie doll to play with, bathe, comb, and dress. Some think it's their ticket to regular welfare checks. And others think that having a baby will remove their loneliness. Is any of that what motherhood is supposed to be all about?

One thing is sure: having a baby means taking on a great responsibility. Babies need to be fed and cared for. They have to grow up, and that takes a long time. And, as they are growing up, they need a father and mother who will stand by them through every stage of maturing. We can't just have children and then give them to their grandmother to be raised, and children also can't raise themselves. Consider what the Bible teaches:

> *Behold, children are a gift of the* L<small>ORD</small>*;*
> *The fruit of the womb is a reward.*
>
> Psalm 127:3, NAS

If you're saved and happily married, that's the only time you should begin to think of having a family. Otherwise, wait on the Lord's timing. It's too great a responsibility otherwise.

A<small>PPLYING</small> <small>FOR</small> L<small>OW</small>-I<small>NCOME</small> H<small>OUSING</small>

I had planned to get an apartment with the money I had saved through years of work at the telephone company. Now, it seemed, I would need it for other things (like furniture). But what good would furniture do us if we had no place to live?

Mama Fedie was working for the New York City Housing

Authority and was familiar with the application procedures there. She suggested that we apply for public housing. We welcomed that idea and were about to apply for some apartments that were available, when a new development suddenly came open.

These apartments were called the Pink Houses. Named for Louis H. Pink, they were experimental apartments, uniquely designed, different from all the other projects, but they were still for low-income families. I was very excited. I certainly didn't want to bring a baby home to a place like Koscuisko Street.

We were placed on a waiting list and given a tentative move-in date. I started counting the months, the weeks, and the days until that date would arrive. At last, we would have everything new—a new baby, a new apartment, new furniture—a whole new life. Alas, our life together was not to be what I had expected.

The Curse of Drink

John began drinking, staying out all night, and doing the craziest things. It got so bad that I decided that, when the day came to move, he would not be moving with me. I packed all my things, sprayed them, and put them outside in the hallway, ready to go to the new place. Still, by the time my labor pains came, I was trapped in that rat-infested apartment.

Fedie Renee Is Ready To Make Her Appearance

Little Fedie Renee couldn't wait to make her arrival, it seems, and the pains continued for several days. Be-

I WILL BLESS THEE

cause it was my first experience, I kept going to the Emergency Room, and they kept sending me home, saying that it wasn't time yet. I was experiencing false labor. I would have to be dilated a certain number of centimeters before they would admit me, so I just needed to walk around more and then come back later.

Toward the end, they had two of us walking around the halls of the hospital like that. The other lady's baby suddenly began to come out, and before they could get her into a delivery room, the head was already visible.

After they got her situation under control, someone remembered me and came out shouting, "Where's that lady who was here a while ago? Admit her!" And they finally took me in. But that was just the beginning of my sorrows.

> *I started counting the months, the weeks, and the days!*

I laid there for the longest time, going through what seemed like unbearable pain, and still the baby wasn't coming. Eventually, they gave me something to induce labor, and the struggle began in earnest.

I Gave That Doctor a Fit

Being as yet unsaved, I wasn't an easy person to deal with. I kicked and screamed and protested, while the doctor and nurses were trying to move the baby down the birth canal. At one point, the doctor positioned himself over my stomach and began pushing downward, trying to coax the baby out. I screamed and kicked and said, "Get off my stomach, you stupid jerk."

"Shut up," he told me.

"Don't tell me to shut up," I argued.

"Push!" he shouted.

I gave that doctor a fit.

PUSH!

This might all seem funny to some, but this is just what we do when God is trying to bring us through some fiery trial. I have a message I minister entitled PUSH. It means Pray Until Something Happens. We're giving birth to ministries, and it's a painful process. If we scream and act out and fail the test, we only have to repeat it again and again, until we can eventually pass.

But this is only a test, and God knows just what you can bear. His Word teaches us:

> *For My yoke is easy and My burden is light.*
> Matthew 11:30, NAS

Trust God, and you will give birth to your destiny.

BORN AT LAST

Fedie Renee was born on March 18, and I was so proud to carry that first little bundle of joy home. She was tiny, just five pounds, five and a half ounces. She had a light brown complexion, and her head was bald. She was my little Redd doll.

Continued Drinking

With the birth of our first child, I had hoped that John would change. He didn't. He continued to drink and to stay out all night. He simply couldn't resist his bottle, and I had seen where he got that habit. Every day, when his sister Susie and her husband Herman came home from work, the first thing they did was take out a bottle of liquor, get a glass out of the cabinet, and start pouring.

I hadn't known that he was a drinker before we married, but then, I never inquired. I was afraid the Lord would take him out of my life, too, so I didn't ask. And this is what I got.

I urge young people everywhere to learn from my mistakes. Inquire about your prospective mate, about their family, their educational background, and, most of all, about their spiritual life. Ask if there has been any past knowledge of Christ as Savior and Lord in the family. Did they attend Sunday school in their youth? Were both parents present in the home? Did they have family prayer? Was there any history of abuse? For example, did your man's father beat, curse, and abuse his wife and/or children? Many sons follow in their father's footsteps.

Does your prospective husband love and respect his mother, or does your prospective wife love and respect her father? If so, he or she will be more inclined to love and respect you. What kind of habits does this person have? Do they drink, even a little? Even then, pray before making any serious move. You owe it to yourself.

If you're unsaved and don't know how to pray, find someone who does know how to get a prayer answered. Then seek God's heart, and ask Him, first of all, to save you. Salvation is the greatest thing you could ever ask Him for. When it comes, it's like a package deal, but greater. You get the Father, the Son, and the Holy Ghost, and it's wonderful living for the Lord. I only wish that I had received Him into my life much earlier and that I had lived for Him my whole life.

As the old familiar hymn says:

> *What a friend we have in Jesus,*
> *All our sins and grief to bear,*
> *What a privilege to carry*
> *Everything to God in prayer,*
> *Oh, what peace we often forfeit,*
> *Oh, what needless pain we bear;*
> *All because we do not carry*
> *Everything to God in prayer.*

Chapter Six
They Hated Knowledge

*For that they hated knowledge, and did not choose the fear of the L*ORD*: they would none of my counsel: they despised all my reproof. Therefore shall they eat of the fruit of their own way, and be filled with their own devices.* Proverbs 1:29-31

Because of my upbringing, I knew to consult my mother before making certain decisions. Her prayers had kept me from many heartaches. This time, I was on my own, and I was soon reaping the fallout from my unwise actions.

John's Job

I was very impressed when the Rockefeller Foundation in New York City gave John a job, and the Housing Authority was able to calculate our monthly rental on his income alone. It was a good organization, with excellent benefits, and they seemed to like John. He was dedicated to his position, that of stock clerk, and he made people laugh—when he was sober.

When they notified us that we were on the waiting list for Pink Houses and that our building would be one of the first to open, I was very excited. Because we couldn't qualify for low-income housing with our combined incomes, I resigned from my position at the New York Telephone Company and stayed home with the baby.

But some men seem to be afraid of responsibility. All John had to do now was pay a small monthly rent and buy us some groceries, and if he had managed his money well, he could have easily done that. But, even after we moved and got a new start, he kept drinking, staying out all night, and coming in acting like a fool. Worse yet, he was not bringing his money home.

Our Lovely Apartment

With the money I had saved, I bought all new furniture. It was absolutely gorgeous. I remember especially the mauve sectional, with silver strands running through it, and the orange chair, with the matching ottoman. I also had beautiful glass-topped end tables and a matching coffee table. I kept about three coats of wax on my floors, and they were beautiful and shiny.

Because it was built differently, there were many Jews and Italians, and people of other nationalities living in that housing project. Our apartment was near the eleva-

THEY HATED KNOWLEDGE

tor, so our neighbors often peeped into it. "Oh, yes!" they would say. "It's just as beautiful as they said." I had acquired a taste for excellence from Mama Fedie, and my apartment was on constant display.

MY MAN HAD ALL OF THE PROPER QUALIFICATIONS, BUT ...

I had married a man with all the qualifications I'd always thought I needed, but my marriage to him had turned out to be a very bad choice. It's much more important that a man has (and knows how to exercise) common sense than that he look good. I had never thought about this fact before I said yes to John's proposal. When I got the package, to my dismay, it came with many flaws.

> *My marriage to him had turned out to be a very bad choice!*

I had chosen a light-skinned man with pretty hair, but what does that have to do with marriage? In time, I was forced to apply for an order of protection, because my man didn't know how to treat me. When he had been drinking, he became violent, and all he could think about was "messing up" my face. Thank God that His grace and mercy brought me through it all. But we were separated more than we were together. Still,

It took years of abuse before I finally decided that something had to change.

WAS HAVING ANOTHER CHILD THE ANSWER?

At one point, I thought that perhaps the answer was to have another child. "Lord, please give me another daughter," I prayed, "so that Renee can have someone to grow up with, and so that each of the children can let me know when the other is doing something wrong." There was another reason I wanted another child. It was obvious to me that this man and I would not be together much longer, and this might be my last chance to have a child.

Even though I was not serving the Lord, He honored my plea, and I became pregnant again. This time, I had no morning sickness, so I was able to do temporary work. As with the first pregnancy, I didn't show much. My babies grew in my hips.

TIME FOR MORE PAIN

When the time came to deliver, I was determined that I would not suffer the pain I'd had with my first child. Somewhere I'd heard that if you had a heart condition of any kind, doctors would give you something for the pain. I told the attending doctor that I had a heart murmur. (I had been diagnosed as having a heart murmur when I was still very young, but if I really had it, it had never bothered me.) The doctor noted this in my records, and when the delivery date came, they had the needed pain medicine in place.

THEY HATED KNOWLEDGE

Some of us don't want to go through anything. We take tranquilizers, aspirin, and painkillers of every stripe, instead of praying. But these are not the answer. The answer is PUSH: Pray Until Something Happens! I've been there, so I know what I'm talking about.

PUSH Some More

This baby came much faster than the first. After they drugged me, I was very relaxed ... until I heard the doctor say to me, "Mother, wake up! You've got to help bring this baby into the world. Push!"

I could hear myself, as if I were way off in the distance, answering him, "I'm pushing."

We love to be "out of it" so that we don't feel pain, but we never know God in His fullness until we've been through something. Wake up! And go through!

In time, Patricia Lynn came out, eight pounds, four ounces, a pretty girl with a full head of straight, dark-brown hair. But there seemed to be something wrong with her. She cried nonstop for the first few months of her life. She had something doctors call "colic," a condition babies suffer when exposed to air during delivery. Eventually she got over it, but it was a terrible trial for us in the meantime.

I Became a Keypunch Operator

When the girls were of age, I was able to get them into daycare, and I began looking for a job. Since I'd worked at the telephone company and had a few hours of keypunch operation and some other machinery, I put this all on my resume. In no time at all, I had more job offers than I could fill. Some jobs I remember more than others, but there was one in particular.

I was hired at top salary, but then I had difficulty doing the job. I was making so many mistakes that the girl verifying my work didn't know what to do. This made me very nervous, because I needed the work to take care of my girls.

I know that Mama was praying for me, and I must inject here a few words of a song:

> *I went on from that job to supervising the night shift at Franklin Simon's office complex!*

And when I think of her, so dear,
 I feel her gentle presence near,
Her voice comes floating on the air,
Reminding me of Mother's prayer.

My situation made me bold enough to go to the manager who had hired me and complain. I told him that the person verifying my work had made me nervous and caused me to make a lot of mistakes. He immediately called for the night supervisor.

"Bertha," he said, "Gwen tells me that she's very unhappy on your shift. What's the problem?"

THEY HATED KNOWLEDGE

"She just doesn't know how to key punch," she said. She was thinking that I was going to get fired, and I was too. Instead, the manager called the day supervisor and told her to work with me and teach me everything I needed to know about the job. Within a few days, she reported back to him that I no longer needed her help. God's favor was upon me.

On to Greater Things

I went on from that job to supervising the night shift at Franklin Simon's office complex, and promotions kept on coming. One night, one of my employees, a lady who loved to talk on the phone, had to be reprimanded. Her boyfriend called and threatened to kill me, if I fired her. I told the manager about it, and he fired her the next night. This made me a bit nervous, because I'd heard that her boyfriend had only recently gotten out of jail. I needed another job, and I found it supervising the IBM Department at Honeywell Computer Division.

Learning About Sexual Fulfillment

While things were going so well for my professional life, they were not going so well at home. When John was home, he continued drinking, staggering into the apartment, wanting to fight. His abuse became unbearable. He claimed it was all my fault, because, he said, I was "the coldest woman" he'd ever met. This was an excuse to deny what the real problem was: his drinking. He had to blame someone (besides himself), and I was the target of choice.

TRIED IN THE FIRE

To this point in life, I'd had no idea there was such a thing as sexual fulfillment for women. All I knew of marriage was that a woman was to make a man's meals, keep his house clean, and have his children. Sex was just a duty that had to be performed. It was John's cousin's wife, Thelma, who first told me that sex between a married man and woman was intended to be something wonderful. I wasn't experiencing that, so I was curious and wanted to find out why.

Now I knew that John was failing me, and I thought I knew why he was trying to blame me instead. But, when I tried to talk to him about it, none of it made sense to him. His mind was so "messed up" that all he wanted to do was beat me up.

For my part, I began to think that I needed to search for someone to fill the void in my life. I wanted to see if I was as "cold" as John was accusing me of being.

I Finally Met My Dream Man

I met Rudy through one of my girlfriends in the Bronx. He worked for General Motors, made good money, and was tall, dark, and handsome. He was about six feet, two inches tall, had an ebony brown complexion, and had dark brown wavy hair. He weighed about two hundred and fifty pounds. In short, Rudy was a hunk, if there ever was one. (Here we go again ... attracted to a man because of his looks. Would I never learn?)

I had to stand on top of the stairs to kiss Rudy goodnight, and I just knew that I'd found my ideal man.

THEY HATED KNOWLEDGE

He seemed to be everything I needed, lovingly warm, affectionate, tender, and kind. He would never abuse a woman, by getting drunk, choking her around her neck, and cursing her out (all things that I was constantly suffering with John). No, Rudy was the kind of man who could just take you in his arms and melt you. This is what I'd been looking for, so I was convinced that I didn't need to look any further. Suddenly, my life was totally wrapped up in this man.

Wrapped Up in a Man

Ladies, I beg of you: please never get wrapped up in a man. Our God has said:

You shall have no other gods before Me.
Exodus 20:3, NAS

That includes a man. Our God is a jealous God, and when we worship our boyfriends, girlfriends, husbands, wives, children, or anything or anybody more than Him, that's a definite no-no. God will go so far as to move people out of your life, if and when He sees that you love them more than Him. So, please take my advice.

All of you women who are praying for a husband, please answer this one question: If he said to you, "Honey, stay at home with me today, and don't go to church," what would you say? It's an important question.

Sometimes we wonder why we can't seem to get a decent proposal. It's because we're not ready for it. If it happened, you'd put the Lord on the back burner, just for that man, and then claim it was God who told you to do it. Once you're married, you cannot please the Lord in the same way as you can when you're single. Then, your first duty is to your husband. God's Word says:

> *There is difference also between a wife and a virgin. The unmarried woman careth for the things of the Lord, that she may be holy both in body and in spirit: but she that is married careth for the things of the world, how she may please her husband.*
> 1 Corinthians 7:34

Whatever your state, be true to God.

Should I Marry Rudy?

In time, Rudy asked me to marry him, and I knew that I had a very serious decision to make. On the one hand, I knew what I wanted, but on the other hand, I also knew what was right. I was a married woman, and this man was not my legal husband.

Then again, Rudy loved me as I had always wanted to be loved, and this made me feel very good. At the same time, my legal husband was a total jerk who seemed only to want to hurt me. Should all of that be grounds for a change?

While I was trying to get an answer to this quandary, John came over one night to the place we were staying, driven by the devil himself. There he took a whole bottle

THEY HATED KNOWLEDGE

of sleeping tablets and then started staggering around the house. I was afraid for him, and, when I couldn't get an ambulance fast enough, I drove him to King's County Hospital myself.

While John was waiting to be seen, he became impatient and climbed over the railing of the bed. His behavior was so erratic that the doctors there decided to admit him to a mental institution on Long Island. He was to remain there under observation, for the next three months. Rudy paid limousine service for me to go out there and visit John, so I went every Sunday and took him food and anything else I could.

But now Rudy grew impatient. He would give me three weeks to make a decision about our future together—or else. Would I agree to divorce John

> *I knew that I had a very serious decision to make!*

and to fly to Las Vegas and marry him? (He was willing to take care of all the expenses.) Or would he be forced to walk out of my life and never look back?

It was a terrible moment. I knew that I loved this man. He had given me sexual fulfillment and financial security, and yet something within me made me refuse his offer. I already had a husband, and I must be faithful to him—however low he had sunk. I didn't believe in divorce and had never believed in divorce. I had made a vow before God, and I must keep that vow.

That was my decision, and it caused Rudy to do exactly what he had promised: He walked out of my life and never looked back.

I rode the train to the Bronx that night, looking for him, and I found him. I told him that I was addicted to his kind of love and care, and that I needed him to hold me in his arms and let me know that everything was going to be all right. He did hold me that night, but that was the last time it was to be. I was devastated.

My Life Was in Ruins

After Rudy walked out of my life, I became a nervous wreck. I had to take nerve pills every four hours and Sominex to sleep at night. My nose twitched, and one eye jumped. The doctor said I would need a year's supply of Vitamin B Complex to restore my nervous system.

I was in some hospital every year for something. I would choose the hospital in advance, based on how modern it was, what kind of food they served, and what area of town it was in. It had to be a private hospital, because I had good insurance to cover the room and the doctor. I had a medicine cabinet full of all kinds of medicines. Just name an ailment, and I could prescribe something for it.

God's Ultimatum

This went on for some time, until one day I received the Lord's ultimatum. I heard Him say, "If you don't live

THEY HATED KNOWLEDGE

for Me, you're not going to live." Some people don't believe that the Lord speaks to us today, but I feel sorry for them.

When I heard the Lord say that, I began to count the cost. There is always a price to be paid to follow God. It may cost you boyfriends. It may cost you bad habits. It may mean that you'll be alone for a time and celibate. For my part, I had to give up everything that wasn't pleasing to God.

Part of that commitment was to renounce sex apart from marriage. Sex can be wonderful within marriage, but sex is not the be-all many make it out to be.

Marriage (even a happy marriage) can exist without sex. What happens when your husband becomes impotent? Do your wedding vows still mean anything? When you married him, you said:

> *For better or for worse,*
> *In sickness or in health,*
> *Until death us do part.*

Can your love stand the test of time? Real love always finds a way:

Love is patient, love is kind and is not jealous; love does not brag and is not arrogant.

1 Corinthians 13:4, NAS

But I hadn't yet learned for myself what I'm, even now, preaching to you through these pages. I just knew that I had to make a change in my life.

TRIED IN THE FIRE

MY FINANCIAL WOES

After Rudy, instead of life getting better, it had somehow gotten worse. Because Rudy had been taking care of me while John was in the hospital, John had told his boss not to release any money to me, and he didn't. I was sure that when John came home, he would give me back the money I had paid out for household needs, but when he came out and got his money, he threw parties instead, wasting his money on riotous living. He gave me nothing. Needless to say, I was extremely upset by this, thinking that this was the thanks I received for deciding to stand by my man. Perhaps I had made a wrong choice after all.

I hadn't. God said:

> *A new thought began to take form in my mind!*

For we know in part and we prophesy in part; but when the perfect comes, the partial will be done away.
1 Corinthians 13:9-10, NAS

At first, I couldn't believe that I had, at long last, found the man of my dreams and then let him get away from me. I had thought I was looking for love in a man, but I found out that what I was really looking for was a way to fill an empty void in my life, and that, of course, was my need for Jesus. I needed to get to church, where I could find Him.

SEEKING FOR A NEW LOVE

Even as I planned to go to church, a new thought began to take form in my mind. I had often ridden the New Lots Avenue bus, and it had a very handsome driver. For a long time now, he had been flirting with me, asking me out, and I had refused. Now, I decided that I would give in to him, meet him after work some day, and go out with him. I rationalized this away, by telling myself that I just wanted to prove, one more time, that John was wrong. I was not the coldest woman around.

I actually had the nerve to call John and ask him to come over and stay with the girls, while I went to church (to meet a bus driver). In all honesty, I was not nearly as interested in church as I was in that man.

I dressed in my navy blue suede and leather suit, with navy blue shoes and a bag to match. I even had a royal blue hat, with blue accessories. I was looking sharp that night, and could only imagine what effect it would have on the driver. To my dismay, when I boarded the bus that night, he was not the driver.

I felt betrayed and humiliated. I had somehow built up in my mind the idea that this man could meet my needs, and now, he, too, was gone.

Looking back on it, I now understand that this was all the Lord's doing. If I had found what I needed in a man again, I wouldn't have accepted Jesus as Lord and Savior of my life. In reality, I had lost nothing, compared to finding Jesus. He satisfies my every longing. His grace is sufficient for me. In Him, my strength is made perfect in weakness. Oh, how I love Him! But that was all to come later. At the moment, I was totally dismayed.

I went on to church, having chosen to attend Bishop F.D. Washington's Memphis Drive service. All the while, I was planning to meet the driver on my way back home.

When I got to the church, I was surprised to find that Sister Ernestine Cleveland was the speaker. I had heard a lot about her and had even one time said to the Lord many years before, "I think if You would send Sister Ernestine Cleveland to our church, I'd get saved." Well, here I was, and here she was! What now?

I listened to her testimony, but I had no desire to give myself to the Lord that night. All I could think about was meeting that driver on the bus on my way home. My life had degenerated to this very low level. But all that was about to change. And quickly!

Chapter Seven

Speak, for Thy Servant Heareth

And the L<small>ORD</small> came, and stood, and called as at other times, Samuel, Samuel. Then Samuel answered, Speak; for thy servant heareth.   1 Samuel 3:10

When Sister Ernestine Cleveland had finished her message, she didn't ask, as is customary, for those who wanted to be saved to come forward. Instead, she said simply, "Anyone who is not saved, stand to your feet." Wow! What should I do now?

I Couldn't Lie in Church

Mama had taught us the story of how Ananias and Sapphira had lied to the Holy Ghost and then dropped dead before the entire church, so I wasn't about to lie in church. The woman of God had said for those who were not yet saved to stand up, so I had no choice. I had to stand up. There was no way to escape it.

I stood up, and then she asked those of us who were standing to move toward the altar. I did this too.

As I was standing there at the altar with the rest of the group, I heard a voice saying, "If you give your heart to Me, I'll move that old mean boss." Nobody at that altar knew that I had a mean boss. In fact, nobody in the church even knew me at all. Suddenly, I found myself throwing up my hands and saying, "Yes, Lord!" Then, I started to dance and to jump up and down. I was so happy. The void I had long needed filled was suddenly satisfied.

> *"If you give your heart to Me, I'll move that old mean boss!"*

The young ladies who prayed with me at the alter later told me they wondered how I could dance in the Spirit standing up. When they tried it, they always lost their balance and fell. Many, who were coming out of denominational churches in those days, fainted in the Spirit, and had to be given smelling salts to revive. I was moving in the Spirit.

Sharing the Good News

I had totally forgotten the man on the bus (whom I had planned to meet afterward). Instead, my first thought was to call Mama, as soon as I got home, and tell her that I had gotten saved. I knew she would be overjoyed, as she had prayed for me constantly for all those years.

"Mama," I said excitedly, the minute I heard her voice on the other end of the line, "I just got saved and filled with the Holy Ghost." She was overjoyed.

"Did you speak in tongues?" she asked.

"Well, I think so," I said, so excited and joyful about what had just happened that I hardly knew which end was up.

"Go back to the altar and make sure you're filled," she said. And then, as if to cement it in my mind, she repeated it: "Go back to the altar and get filled."

Filled with the Holy Ghost

I went back to the meeting the next night, and the saints tarried with me for a long time. When I didn't receive, they told me to come back the next night. This time, the Lord led me to fast and pray. I was determined to be filled with the Holy Ghost. When I went back again, I was dead serious.

Toward the end of the service, just when people were beginning to leave the altar, I began to speak with other tongues, and somebody (it could have been Mother Washington), announced to everyone, "She just received the baptism of the Holy Ghost." What joy filled my soul! What peace filled my mind!

I called Mama back that night and told her the good news, that I'd been filled with the Holy Ghost, and we rejoiced together over the telephone.

God Kept His Promise

Not many days after that, the Lord kept His promise ... and more. The supervisor who was directly over me was moved, my old mean boss was fired, and the boss over him was transferred to New England. That had to be God. He was helping me.

Eventually, I left Honeywell and took a position with the IBM Corporation. I thought I wanted to work part time, so that I could come and go as I pleased, but I found myself getting very involved in witnessing on the job to people the Lord led me to. This proved to be the way I grew.

Saints, if *you* want to grow in God, start to witness to those the Lord leads you to. What a blessing it is, not only to the one receiving the witness, but even more so, to the one giving the witness!

Following the Woman of God

Because I had been saved under Evangelist Ernestine Cleveland's ministry, I loved to go to churches where she was ministering. I even traveled to Philadelphia to meet her. It was there in Philadelphia that I met a mighty prayer warrior named Mrs. Erma Morris. She was to become my spiritual mother.

My Spiritual Mom

Erma Morris was not easy to get close to, for she didn't make friends easily. One day, when the two of us were visiting a church together, I prayed that God would give her a burden for me and cause her to have a special love for me. During that service, I had the opportunity to reach over and pray for her. Her legs were giving her pain. The Lord healed her instantly, and through that, we became fast friends.

My girls and I began spending weekends with Sister Erma and her husband. It seemed natural to call them Mom and Pop. They were parents to me and grandparents to my girls, and that proved important, for shortly after that, Mama went home to be with the Lord. Daddy remarried and moved to California. So I'm not sure what I would have done without Mom and Pop Morris.

My First Serious Fast

I had been called by God, and now there was to be a time of preparation. Since I had been saved only a few days before the start of the annual Convocation in Memphis, I longed to go. Instead, I stayed home that year and sought the Lord in fasting and prayer for three days. I thought I was fasting along with many others, since the church held a National Fast. I later learned that the National Fast was the following week. Nevertheless, my fast gave me a great start on my spiritual life. I was anointed immediately to begin my journey of faith.

Through the Waters of Baptism

I received the Lord in October, and I put my name on a list to be baptized. When the night came for the baptismal service, it was very cold. I will never forget that very special night. I came out of the water chilled in my body, but on fire in my soul. I had fulfilled this special ordinance instituted by Christ Himself, and I was on my way to greater things.

Attending the Convocation

The following year, I made plans to go for the Convocation and take the girls with me. We rode with someone else, and, for me, it was a very trying trip. When I had taken the train from Memphis to New York and back again, it had traveled on all of the flat land. This time, we drove through the mountains, and all the ups and downs frightened me. I prayed a lot in the back seat. The route through the mountains was totally unfamiliar to me, and it was, after all, a twenty-four hour trip in all. We arrived in Memphis with a powerful anointing because of our prayers through the mountains, but I promised myself that I would never again make the trip by car.

The next year, I began telling my associates early on that I intended to fly to Memphis. They knew that I didn't have much money, as a single parent, but Bishop Washington preached faith to us, and after hearing his messages, we felt that we could conquer the world.

As the time grew near for the Convocation, the ladies I worked with would ask me if I had gotten my airline tickets yet. "Not yet," I told them, "but I know I'll get them." A few weeks before the Convocation, a man called me to say that he had read an article in *Ebony* magazine that said you could now charge airline flights on credit cards. I hadn't known that fact. I went to American Airlines and charged three round-trip tickets to Memphis. I could later pay it off in installments. It was my first flight.

An Unpleasant Flight

It was not a pleasant flight. We encountered such severe turbulence that passengers were screaming and crying in fear. I asked the Lord why I felt so calm. Why was it that this very turbulent ride seemed smooth to me and the girls? "Gwen," He said, "you will be flying often in the future. If you were to give in to fear on this flight, you might never want to fly again. Instead, I will give you calm in the midst of the storm."

In the future, I was to fly, not only to many parts of this country, but also to many other countries, and the Lord would always be with me.

CHAPTER EIGHT

HIS PRAISE IN JERUSALEM

For he hath looked down from the height of his sanctuary; from heaven did the LORD behold the earth; to hear the groaning of the prisoner; to loose those that are appointed to death; to declare the name of the LORD in Zion, and his praise in Jerusalem. Psalm 102:19-21

Shortly after attending the Convocation, I received a strong desire to visit Jerusalem, the Holy City. I called El Al, Israel's Airlines, to ask what the round-trip fare was to Jerusalem, and they told me it was $999.00. I was saddened by that. Surely it would take me a lifetime to save up that kind of money right then.

ANOTHER OPPORTUNITY

Some months later, the secretary of our church, Sister Catherine Brown, told me one day that she was taking a group of people on a trip to five different countries, and the trip included Jerusalem. I asked her how much the trip would cost, and she told me $1,500.00. Oh my, it was getting worse! If I couldn't raise $999.00, how could I raise $1,500.00? She suggested that I might want to finance the trip with a vacation loan from Citi-Bank, and she gave me an application. I sent in the application, and it was approved. I was off to Jerusalem.

As it turned out, there were only three of us on that trip: Sister Catherine Brown, Sister Lillian Rogers, and myself. When Lillian's father (Bishop Rogers) came to the airport to see us off, he told someone that we were going to visit eight countries. I responded, "I claim it!" I was full of faith and believed that God could do anything. He could ... and He did.

An Expanded Itinerary

The itinerary for the trip read Sweden, Switzerland, Israel, Holland, and England. The first stop the plane made was in Bergen, Norway. We only stayed there a few hours, but that was an extra country.

The next stop was Copenhagen, Denmark. That was a second extra country.

At some point, the comment was made that we were near Germany, and I said, "Lord, I wonder what it's like in Germany." On our way into Switzerland, our plane started to make a rumbling noise, and began ascending and descending like a roller coaster. Something was clearly

HIS PRAISE IN JERUSALEM

wrong, and I started praying. The last thing I wanted was to die in an airplane crash so far from home. Eventually, the turbulence subsided, and we landed.

Our flight attendant took the microphone to announce that we had gone through a very strong storm, and it had forced us to be diverted to Frankfort, Germany. We had missed the last connecting flight into Switzerland, but the airlines would be putting us up in hotel rooms for the night. I was overjoyed. "Yes, Lord," I said. We were in the third extra country.

We were taken to one of the most beautiful hotels in Frankfurt, and each of us was given a separate room. The rooms were plush, with beautiful white feather comforters, snow white pillows, gorgeous mahogany furniture, and a big bathtub that looked like our whirlpool tubs of today. They were shaped like a bathtub, but they were much deeper, and there was some blue bubble bath to relax us while in the tub.

> *The itinerary for the trip read Sweden, Switzerland, Israe, Holland, and England!*

On our pillows, we found miniature blocks of German chocolate candy. God knew about our every need and also about our wants.

TRIED IN THE FIRE

THE NIGHT WAS SPOILED

Our rooms had large keys, almost like those used to open jail cells. It was such an interesting place, and we should have had a wonderful time. Instead, I tossed and turned all night long.

One of the sisters had told me about a lady she knew who had died in Germany, and, she said, Mahalia Jackson had gotten sick there too. We began to wonder if what had looked like chocolate on the pillow had really been poison. All that long restless night, I kept thinking about what she had said and couldn't rest.

What a shame! Never allow anyone to throw a damper on the things you've received because of your faith. Instead, rejoice in everything that God provides.

FIRST CLASS TO ISRAEL

We went on to spend a couple of days in Switzerland and, from there, we were headed to Jerusalem. I said, "Lord, I've never flown first class. I wonder what it would be like." No sooner had I said it than it was done. The airline personnel told us that they had overbooked the coach section of the plane, so they would have to put us in first class. We didn't mind that one bit. We sang all the way to Jerusalem, basking in the comforts of first class.

Jerusalem, Jerusalem,
Lift up your gates and sing!
Hosanna in the highest,
Hosanna to our King!

HIS PRAISE IN JERUSALEM

The other passengers, even the ones who were Jewish, were cheering us on, so we sang and glorified the Lord with abandon.

Arriving in the Holy City

My greatest desire, in visiting the Holy City, was to pray in the Upper Room. There were, of course, many other wonderful places to visit. Before we slept, we reserved a taxi to take us out the next morning, and we got up before daylight and headed first to the Wailing Wall. As I knelt down beside that anointed wall, I started to speak in tongues. There were two Jewish ladies praying nearby, and one of them said, "She's Hebrew."

The other lady said, "Leave her alone and let her pray."

The gentleman who was to escort us to the Upper Room said to me, "You spoke in a beautiful Hebrew language." I knew it had to be the Holy Ghost. When I think about it even now, I feel the power of God coming over me.

The Upper Room is nothing fancy. It is situated in a small building, has a simple concrete floor, and is, for the most part, empty. As I knelt on that floor, I felt God's presence and started to weep. Tears streamed down my face, and the Holy Ghost began speaking out of me, ministering to me, empowering me, and inspiring me to win more souls for Christ. Jerusalem was part of my preparation, and it was a glorious one.

We went on to visit other holy sites, but nothing touched

me quite as much as those two places. All too soon, our visit to the land of the Bible was ended, and we boarded our plane for the return trip.

Saints of God, you should desire to go to Jerusalem, the Holy City of God. Walk the stages of the cross, view the empty tomb, and feel the presence of the Lord still there among His people. Pray to do this before the Lord comes back. You will never be the same again.

ON TO HOLLAND

From Jerusalem, we flew to Amsterdam in Holland. What a beautiful country and city that is! Although it rained just about every day we were there, they had the most beautiful flowers I had ever seen. There were canals in the streets, and sightseeing boats traveled up and down them.

We also visited Rotterdam, a few miles away, and saw the most magnificent roses of all colors. Our God made them all.

> *Walk the stages of the cross, view the empty tomb, and feel the presence of the Lord still there among His people!*

HIS PRAISE IN JERUSALEM

While on the trip, we were blessed to be able to witness in a park in Amsterdam. There was a group of young people there from all over Europe, touring the country, and they had a listening ear. When you say yes to the Lord, there is no telling where He may send you.

ENGLAND AND HOME

We left Holland, headed to London, England, and from there, returned home. It was a beautiful trip, and I received an anointing from God that has impacted my life in a mighty way ever since.

MOM MORRIS' MINISTRY TO THE GIRLS

I was go grateful to God that I hadn't had to worry about the girls during the trip. They were in good hands, in Philadelphia, with Mom and Pop Morris. She was a tough disciplinarian, and they thought she was mean, but they also thought I was mean. Anyway, they survived the experience and were the better for it.

Mom Morris was wise. She told the girls that if they received the Holy Ghost, she would take them to Hershey Park. They liked the sound of that, and as a result, they were filled with the Holy Ghost, speaking in tongues. Renee even began to pray for the sick, and they were healed. Thank God.

Chapter Nine

Free Indeed

If the Son therefore shall make you free, ye shall be free indeed.   John 8:36

After I had gotten saved, John asked if he could come home. I knew I was changed, and I was praying that he would change too. Later, I would come to the conclusion that allowing him to come back home before he changed was a mistake. It wasn't long before he was back to his old tricks.

God doesn't expect us to live in a relationship with an abusive man, and if you insist on staying in such a relationship, it just might kill you. Aside from the physical damage a man can do to a woman, you might develope high blood pressure and have a stroke, get cancer or some other type of sickness, all because of the stresses that man keeps you under. Don't let that happen. Run for your life! I speak from experience.

READY TO DIE

One Christmas Eve, John came home drunk and began to beat on me. He forced me under the coffee table in the living room and had his hands around my neck, choking me. Because I was saved now and tired of getting beaten, I decided to just give up and let him kill me. Maybe my death would be the thing that would bring about his salvation. I even prayed that way: "Lord, if he'll be saved through my death, take me on to Heaven right now."

> *Maybe my death would be the thing that would bring about his salvation!*

About that time, I heard a voice saying, "Get up from there!"

I bit my husband, and he jumped back and stopped choking me. I was able to push him away, and I ran out the door and down the stairway.

I called Mama and told her what had happened. She said, "Call a policeman. The law is for the lawless."

I called the police, and they came out, but they were reluctant to arrest John on Christmas Eve.

He eventually went to sleep, but he slept with his

arms around both girls, hoping to prevent me from taking them and leaving. I prayed that the Lord would make him sleep so soundly that I could take them, and he wouldn't know it.

When I thought that he was deep enough in sleep, I whispered to the girls to get up and come with me. They obeyed. I quickly gathered up all the Christmas things I could and ran out of the house with them. A good friend, Terry Richardson, picked us up and took us to her home.

Go Home!

The bed Terry prepared for us seemed to be made of iron. My face, neck, back, and torso were bruised and swollen, and I spent the night in terrible pain. I cried out, "Lord, do You even know that I'm here?"

He answered, "Yes, I know you're there."

"What should I do?" I asked Him.

"Go back," He answered.

"Go back where?" I asked.

He said, "Go home."

I surely had not expected the Lord to send me back to the place where I'd almost lost my life, but I obeyed Him. I went home and fixed a big Christmas dinner and served my family.

Help from a Man of God

My neighbor from across from me, Evangelist Loretta Green, invited me to go to church with her that day. She belonged to Elder Shambach's church in Brooklyn, and I went with her, principally because she told me that her pastor would be willing to talk with me and help me.

I went into the elder's office and told him about my situation. He gave me a card with some biblical encouragement on it, and then he prayed a powerful prayer: "I rebuke the demons in that man and cast them out, in the name of Jesus Christ of Nazareth."

When I got home that night, I tiptoed into the house, trying to keep John from hearing me. He turned over, seemingly on the verge of waking up. I lifted my hands up over his head and prayed, and he went back to sleep and didn't wake up until morning. The next day, he went to work without saying a word about the altercation. What power there is in our God!

The same evangelist advised me to write to other ministers, Brother Al and Brother Epley, asking for prayer, but I had been fasting and praying and didn't feel like bothering anybody else with my situation. Instead, I decided to trust God.

I Was on God's Wheel

I desperately wanted to move out of the projects. I was being faithful to my church, and I knew that faithfulness to God and faith in His promises would cause me to inherit all that He had promised. It would be manifested through obedience and faith in His Word. I had become a witness to the fact that what He says, He will do—and more.

In the meantime, the Lord had me on His wheel,

and since He was then and still is the Potter, we just need to be still and know that He is God. He taught us in His Word that He knows how to *"stablish, strengthen, and settle [us]"*:

> *But the God of all grace, who hath called us unto his eternal glory by Christ Jesus, after that ye have suffered a while, make you perfect, stablish, strengthen, settle you.* 1 Peter 5:10

God was doing a work in me.

SPECIFIC MINISTRIES SOWED INTO MY LIFE

Bishop Washington brought in evangelists from all over the country. One of them, by the name of Evangelist Gilbert Earl Patterson (now our Presiding Bishop), came often to Washington Temple and preached a powerful Gospel to the saints. We young people especially loved it when he came to town. A man of many talents, he also played the organ in those days.

He was still single then, but now he has a beautiful wife, Lady Louise Patterson. He was then and still is a man of fasting and prayer. He has suffered much illness in recent years, and I'm glad that our prayers were answered and that God left him here. We love him.

I cannot forget two other women who helped to shape my life. Men and women of God of this generation, don't throw away the seniors, the fathers and mothers among you. They have a wealth of knowledge that can shape your life.

Mothers Cook and Cunningham (the CC Sisters, as I called them) were two women who helped me grow in God. They taught us holiness. They were powerful teachers of the Gospel, and they demonstrated to us how to be a part of the chosen of the Lord. I can never forget their message on Gideon's three hundred. It was so powerful, and it made each of us want to be part of God's chosen.

My Beginnings in Soulwinning

One Sunday, Bishop Washington announced that a man of God was coming to Washington Temple to teach soulwinning. His name was Evangelist John D. Lawrence. At the time, I wasn't interested in that. I had my mind centered on teaching Sunday school. So, I decided that I would not be able to go until Friday night. That was youth night, and I was in the youth department, so I had to be there that night.

When I finally met this man, his wife, Missionary Ethel Bernice Lawrence, and their six sons and one daughter, I was very impressed. They were all a part of this man's ministry. That night, Evangelist Lawrence did a complete review of everything he had taught from Tuesday through Thursday. I think he did that just for me.

When he discussed door-to-door witnessing (knocking on people's doors, to ask if they were saved or wanted to accept Jesus as Savior), he decided to do a little skit to demonstrate his technique, and I was very surprised and pleased to be selected from the audience to become his silent partner in the skit (the prayer partner). Together, we went out to knock on doors.

I liked this family so much that I felt bad for not having gone to church the other nights. I was planning to attend on Saturday, so I volunteered to meet at the church and go with an actual witnessing group. It was the most wonderful experience I'd ever had. People opened their doors and listened to our presentations, and many accepted Christ as Lord and Savior. We were so excited about the results that we rushed back to the church and fell on our knees with joy and thanksgiving. We were so grateful to God that we had been chosen to bring souls into His Kingdom.

> *We rushed back to the church and fell on our knees with joy and thanksgiving!*

I was asked if I could be the leader of a permanent witnessing team that would go out every Saturday. I had to take time to pray about that, because I was still newly saved and wanted to get God's approval before attempting any type of leadership.

TRIED IN THE FIRE

THE ABUSE CONTINUED

In the meantime, while I was growing in the Lord, I continued to be a victim of physical and verbal abuse. Once John slapped me in the face so hard that I thought his fingerprints would be left there permanently. He just looked at me and asked, "What did Jesus have to say about *that*?"

On another occasion, we were walking together, and he reached over and started to slap me. He stumbled, almost falling, and said "You think *the Lord* did that, don't you?" I didn't answer him.

Many times, he threw our food down the incinerator. I just kept on praying.

He staggered into the church one night and pulled me away from the altar, while I was in prayer. The saints who witnessed this were concerned. I got up quietly, poured some oil on his head, and went outside with him. He eventually calmed down.

Another time, the children and I had taken a train to church, and we were surprised to see their father board the same train. He was drunk, and I was concerned for the children. When he was like that, they were afraid of him. They were nervous, and when he reached out to grab them, they started crying.

Just then, we arrived at the East New York Subway Station. The three of us quickly ran out of the train and up the stairs to the Canarsie Train, waiting with open doors. We jumped on, and the train pulled out of the station. Looking out the window, I saw John staggering up the stairs, too late to stop us.

At the next station, we caught another train going back the other way. When we passed the place where John was still waiting, I bent down so that he couldn't see me. We went to church another way. Once again, God had made a way of escape for us.

Kill Him

Eventually, I got so sick of all this that I asked the Lord to kill him. After all, he was always drunk, cursing us out, beating us, and disrupting our lives. "You should kill him, Lord," I said, and I meant it.

But the Lord answered me, "I'm not going to kill him."

"Why not?" I asked.

"Because you must learn to love him," was His answer.

"Love who, Lord?" I asked.

"John Redd," He told me.

After the Lord said this, I began saying "I love you" to my husband, and I realized that I really did love him. I didn't like the things he did, but I did love his soul. I decided to do a fifty-day fast leading up to Pentecost to break, once and for all, this demonic power that tormented us all. I can never forget what happened.

My Fifty-Day Fast for Deliverance

Three days before the end of the fast, Mother Wells announced one day, "Saints, the Lord spoke to me and told me to tell you to go through."

TRIED IN THE FIRE

I said to myself "Go through what?"

She said. "Go through three days of fasting."

John was a good cook, and when I got home that day, he was there and had baked a chicken for us. When I smelled that, my resolve left me, and I decided to eat. But, no sooner had I agreed to eat than John turned from Dr. Jekyll into Mr. Hyde. I quickly lost my appetite and decided to fast after all.

I made it through the three days of fasting, and the chicken tasted better that Sunday than I imagined it would have that Friday night. I knew that God was going to do something wonderful after that fast, and He did.

> *Lord, You're not moving fast enough to suit me on this matter!*

THE RELEASE

Right after that, John got drunk one night and started to shout at me. He came toward me, as if to hit me. I had a tall, colorful glass vase that sat on the floor of our living room, and I picked it up, intending to hit him with it. I suppose, in my mind, I was saying, "Lord, You're not moving fast enough to suit me on this matter. Maybe I should take things into my own hands." The next thing I remember was me sobbing and praying, "Lord, save me! Save me! Save me!"

My hands trembled, as I cried out to the Lord.

This frightened John, for he had never seen me so distraught. I told him that if he would leave on his own volition, leaving his door keys behind and never coming back, I wouldn't call the police. Otherwise, I would. He left.

The next thing I heard was that he had left New York and gone to California with another woman. The girls knew where he was, because they sometimes spoke with him by phone.

Once, when Patricia was speaking with him, she asked me to take the receiver. He had something he wanted to say to me. I listened tentatively.

"Honey," he said, "I want to come home. I don't want to die like my cousin Fred."

I really didn't know what to say, but I managed to reply, "Whatever the Lord says." I was hoping the Lord would say not to take him back, but if the Lord had said otherwise, I would have obeyed Him. He didn't tell me to take him back.

Financial Victories

Because John had drank up all the money for so long, I was deep in debt, and one day I was praying over our bills, asking the Lord to make a way for me to pay them. "Lord, what good is John Redd?" I prayed. "He doesn't send a dime of support, and here I am struggling in this way."

TRIED IN THE FIRE

A neighbor came to the door to say that there was a telephone call for me (I wasn't able to afford phone service right then). When I went to the phone, it was John's family. He had died in California, they told me. They had tried to bring his body back, but when authorities learned that he had a wife, they insisted that only the wife had the authority to order his body moved.

I made sure that God was glorified at John's funeral. Evangelist John Lawrence preached and made an altar call. It was the first time I had ever attended a funeral where such a thing was done, but it made sense. Funerals are for the living, not for the dead. That day, John's family and friends had the opportunity to receive Jesus as Lord and Savior.

Now that the funeral was over, what next? I remember feeling in my spirit, "If I can just hold on, deliverance will come." It soon did. I remembered having put away two small insurance policies in a file. They had only been worth $25.00 and $5.00 respectively when John first took them out, but they had now matured, and together they were worth more than eleven thousand dollars. What a miracle! I was able to pay my debts.

There was another blessing. Alive, John hadn't been able to take care of his girls, but now his combined Social Security and Veteran's Administration benefits took care of them in his death. He was buried in the Veteran's Cemetery.

There was one more blessing to come. As I said earlier, I had long wanted a home of my own. I was not project material. I had prayed and looked longingly at houses, but our difficult financial circumstances had prevented me from taking any further action. Now, Mama Fedie, who had started selling real estate, called to say that she had seen just the house for me. It wasn't very big, but it would fit the bill.

We went to see it. She was right. It wasn't big. It was more like a doll house. But it could be my house, and that meant a lot to me and the girls. We put a contract on it, and were approved by the bank for a mortgage. How good God is! We must never cease to praise Him.

WOMEN, THINK LONG AND HARD

I praise God for women who have stayed married to men who have abused and misused them, but they must know that God does not require this. I was a stubborn one myself. Ministers would ask me, "Why have you not remarried?"

I would answer "I don't believe in remarrying, as long as my husband is still alive."

Although I did not often wish him dead, I did know that one day he would die, for I knew that God had promised me something better. Now, having gone through all that, I can testify to the truth of the Scriptures:

> *I waited patiently for the* LORD; *and he inclined unto me, and heard my cry.* Psalm 40:1

The Lord admonishes us:

TRIED IN THE FIRE

Be anxious for nothing, but in everything by prayer and supplication with thanksgiving let your requests be made known to God.   Philippians 4:6, NAS

There is one more important thing that I must share with you. It is so very important that we learn not to speak negatively. God has warned:

*Death and life are in the power of the tongue,
And those who love it will eat its fruit.*
                              Proverbs 18:21, NAS

You can actually speak yourself into an early grave. Instead, speak what the Word of God says. Instead of death, decree:

With long life will I satisfy him, and shew him my salvation.   Psalm 91:16

MOVING TOO FAST?

All of this just pushed me higher in the things of the Spirit, and along about this time, Mama was afraid that perhaps I was moving too fast in the Lord. She wanted me to slow down. One of her friends (Mother Gertrude McMullen, who is now 95 years old) told her to leave me alone. God had saved me courageously, she said, and I was moving in Him. Because of this, I was able to freely involve myself in the soulwinning ministry, despite all the obstacles that surrounded my life.

FREE INDEED

How could I do anything else? Our pastor, Bishop Washington, walked, talked, preached, lived, and breathed souls for the Kingdom. He was the inspiration that made us get up off the pews and go out into the hedges and highways, compelling men, women, boys, and girls to seek the Lord.

We are saved to tell others about this glorious Gospel of the Kingdom, so that they, too, can come into the Ark of safety. I was now free to do much more.

Chapter Ten

I Have Chosen You

Ye have not chosen me, but I have chosen you, and ordained you, that ye should go and bring forth fruit, and that your fruit should remain: that whatsoever ye shall ask of the Father in my name, he may give it you. These things I command you, that ye love one another. — John 15:16-17

When I was young, we sang, "I Decided to Make Jesus My Choice," but after learning the truth of John 15:16, I had to change my mind about those words. I was God's choice, not the other way around. Now that I was saved, He had a lot of work to do in me.

We Think We're Ready Before We Are

I have often quoted something I once heard a minister say: "Many were called, few were chosen, and others just went." The Lord has called many to ministry, but too often, we have failed to realize just how much preparation we require.

My husband, the late Bishop F.D. Washington, used to tell the story of a young man who kept telling his pastor that he was called to preach. One night, the pastor randomly called on him to bring the evening message. He stood up and made a complete fool of himself. The pastor said to him, "I thought you told me that the Lord called you to preach."

"Yes, I did," he replied. "But when the Lord heard me preach, He said, 'Never mind.'"

I had been saved and called, and now I had to be prepared.

The Lord First Had to Strip Me

Not long after I got saved, the Lord began to strip me. When I went to church with my earrings and necklaces on, the Lord would let my hand get caught in the necklace, and beads would fly everywhere. Sometimes He would let me get choked on the necklace. Many times, when I wore earrings, I would lose them or at least one of them. I decided to have my ears pierced, so that I wouldn't lose my earrings anymore, but then I developed colloids (big knots) behind my ears. I prayed, and eventually the swelling went away, but I stopped trying to maintain pierced ears.

I also lost one of the most beautiful diamond earrings I ever owned. I had bought them in St. Thomas, but after one was lost, the only thing I could use the other one for was to replace diamonds—if one happened to fall out of my ring.

I also could not wear colored dresses for several years; I only bought white.

During those formative years, I spent a lot of time fasting and praying, working the altar, tarrying with souls who wanted to be saved and filled with the Holy Ghost.

Eventually, the Lord allowed me to go back to wearing my regular clothes, but since then I have realized that I must walk very humbly before God. What the Lord wants to do is to break us, melt us, mold us, and fill us. That's why we sing the chorus, "Spirit of the living God, fall fresh on me."

> *Not long after I got saved, the Lord began to strip me!*

A humbling experience can be hard to take sometimes, but as we noted in an earlier chapter, Jesus said:

> *My yoke is easy, and my burden is light.*
>
>   Matthew 11:30

He also promised not to put any more on us than we can bear:

TRIED IN THE FIRE

There hath no temptation taken you but such as is common to man: but God is faithful, who will not suffer you to be tempted above that ye are able; but will with the temptation also make a way to escape, that ye may be able to bear it.   1 Corinthians 10:13

I have attempted, at all times to be ready for whatever the Lord sends my way, and, as a consequence, there are words, or phrases, that I try never to speak. They are things like, "Lord, I've had enough," or "I can't take anymore." Words like that reflect an inner attitude that can bring about a serious delay in the manifestation of God's promises in our lives.

If we remain faithful through it all, suddenly Heaven bursts in upon us. This is what happened to me one morning.

THE LORD HAD TO CALM MY FEARS

As I was getting ready for work that morning, seemingly everything happened to delay my leaving home on time, and I hated that. I liked to arrive at work at least fifteen to thirty minutes early, so that I could get my coffee and Danish and take my time to eat it before starting my work routine. So, I was mad at the devil, because, as usual, we blame him for everything, and I was sure that he was the cause of me leaving home late.

If my memory serves me correctly, I drove to the Euclid Avenue Subway Station in Brooklyn, parked, and ran for the train. It was late, so I got a seat.

I HAVE CHOSEN YOU

I wasn't in the best frame of mind, but as was my custom, I opened my Bible and began to read it as I traveled. Suddenly, the Lord sat beside me on that train, and He spoke to me from the book of Jeremiah:

Then the word of the Lord came unto me, saying, Before I formed thee in the belly, I knew thee; and before thou camest forth out of the womb I sanctified thee, and I ordained thee a prophet unto the nations. Then said I, Ah, Lord God! behold, I cannot speak; for I am a child. Jeremiah 1:4-6

I was shocked. These were the very words I was about to tell the Lord, for I felt that I had not been saved long enough to merit the favor being visited upon my life. In all reality, I was still a babe in Christ, and yet doors of opportunity were opening to me.

He spoke to me, as He had to Jeremiah:

Say not, I am a child: for thou shalt go to all that I shall send thee, and whatsoever I command thee thou shalt speak. Be not afraid of their faces: for I am with thee to deliver thee, saith the Lord.
Then the Lord put forth his hand, and touched my mouth. And the Lord said unto me, Behold, I have put my words in thy mouth. See, I have this day set thee over the nations and over the kingdoms, to root out, and to pull down, and to destroy, and to throw down, to build, and to plant. Jeremiah 1:7-10

IT STARTED HAPPENING

The youth leader at our church chose me to lead one of the crusaders groups (a team formed for the purpose of witnessing). Usually, as he appointed leaders, he also gave them members, but he gave me none. At first, I cried about this, but when I spoke to him about it, he answered that the Lord would bless me to get some members.

> *To be a soulwinner, you must be chosen by God!*

Then I knew that it was the Lord's doing. To be a soulwinner, you must be chosen by God. If He had chosen me to lead group, He would indeed give me those who were to be members of the group. Before long, the Lord blessed me with four youth crusaders for my team. We had uniforms made (white dresses, with gold capes), and God was with us, as we prepared and then worked.

We were invited by the YPWW field worker, Missionary Thelma Hayes, to come to Kelly Temple in Harlem and witness. This involved passing out tracts and talking to people on the streets. God was with us in an awesome way that day, and many souls were reached. This caused the crusader fame to go far and wide. We were given many opportunities to tell of our experiences in the State

I HAVE CHOSEN YOU

Convocation Youth Night, and many young people became interested in winning souls for Christ.

Witnessing in San Francisco

We worked until a new field worker was appointed. She was Sister Juanita Johnson, and she chartered a plane and flew us to the National Youth Congress in San Francisco. There, we witnessed on the streets of San Francisco and went to a local nursing home and had a service for the patients.

During those days, I was appointed to the financial department for the National Youth Congress, helping with the offering. As the Bible says:

> *A man's gift maketh room for him, and bringeth him before great men.*   Proverbs 18:16

And that's just what happened.

Bishop Washington saw us witnessing in San Francisco, when many others had left the meeting and gone to Los Angeles for sightseeing and other activities. Instead, I had chosen to take that time to minister for the Lord. I said to him that day, "Dad, I like it out here. What would you do if I stayed here?"

He said, "If you want to be out of the will of God, then stay."

That surely burst my bubble. But I was on a spiritual high. I knew now that God had chosen me, perhaps because I had been through so many tests and trying experiences, and they had helped me grow in Him. And, because of it, I had a message.

Turned On to Witnessing

Because I was so turned on to witnessing, I met a young man, during a street meeting in Brooklyn by the name of Elder Milton Rochford. He, too, was hooked on winning the lost at any cost, and now I joined him and his wife, his children, and his younger brother Robert, and we became a team in the soulwinning business. When any door opened to me, I would call him, to see if he was available to share in the ministry. He usually made time to join us, wherever we needed him. He was a singer, pianist/organist, preacher/evangelist, and powerful worker in ministry.

The Beginning of Our Prison Ministry

One day I met someone who was ministering at the Tombs Prison in Manhattan, and they told me about a group that was starting a ministry there. They asked if we were interested, and, without thinking, I said yes. I committed to meeting another lady in New York City early on a Sunday morning, about 7:00 AM to go into the prison.

When the time came, I had changed my mind, but the Lord woke me up early that day, and I headed off to meet the lady. This was to be my first taste of prison ministry, and I wondered what it would be like.

When we walked into that place the first day, it was a

little scary. The chaplain said to us, "Ladies, I must tell you: The men inside this institution are violent, and they could grab one of you and take you hostage. This could even start a riot. If either of you have second thoughts about going into the chapel, you can wait here in the holding area, and when the service is over, we'll all leave together."

When he put it that way, I felt a little hesitancy. What was I getting myself into? Then God gave me His peace and let me know that He would be with us, and we leaned heavily on Him during the entire service.

It was the most powerful service I had ever experienced in any of the places that I'd previously ministered, and the Spirit of the Lord saved, delivered, and set men free that Sunday morning. Consequently, we were very excited. We felt the anointing flowing throughout our very being, and we received another filling of the Holy Ghost. What a mighty God we serve!

After the benediction, they prepared the chapel for the next service, and another group of men came in. This time, we dropped our guard, being excited about the mighty move of God that had come in the first service. Nevertheless, the anointing was upon us just the same, and again men's lives were changed.

The Beginning of Our Hospital Outreach

A year or so later, I met Missionary Norman (now Mother Norman) at First Church, where the late Bishop Frank Clemmons pastored. She was a volunteer at

Goldwater Hospital in New York City. At this Hospital, every patient was in a wheelchair, all victims of crippling diseases or accidents. Now I, Hazel Alexander, Joan Robinson-McDonald, and my two girls, Fedie Renee and Patricia Lynn, joined Mother Norman in ministering there, and many were saved. The chaplain appointed me Volunteer Chaplain for the Friday night service. I played a few little chords on the piano, and so I led some singing and brought the message from God's Word.

Rev. Aaron Brown, an ordained minister, who worked there at the time, also joined us. We were even called upon in the days to come to bury the dead.

During one of the services, a young lady, who was there visiting with her friend (who later became her husband), was saved. She was Delores Hickson (now Delores Jenkins). Delores joined Washington Temple, worked in various auxiliaries in the church, and later became the church secretary. She was the light that drew many of her family members to Christ, and they, too, became members of Washington Temple.

There were two other ladies who ministered with us at Goldwater Hospital, Evangelist Watson and Evangelist Jackie McCullough. Evangelist Jackie was very quiet at that time. I had to prime her up to get her to speak, but that all changed. The last time I was in one of her dynamic services, she asked me, "Would you have ever believed that I would be preaching like I am?"

No, I wouldn't, I had to admit, but many of the souls that God has given me over the years have gone on to become powerful men and women of God.

Not long after I was saved, a dear sister, Mother Elizabeth Ivey, asked me to spend some days with her in her home. She said to me, "Gwen, you are a key person in ministry. You will reach one person, and they will reach thousands." She was a true prophetess of God, for every word she spoke has come to pass.

THE HAMPTON BOYS HOME AND GOSHEN SCHOOL ANNEX

Another opportunity presented itself. The same man who had opened the door for us to the Tombs now inspired us to go and minister to the Hampton Boys Home and Goshen School Annex in upstate New York, and the same group (including my daughters, whom I always took with me in ministry, if children were welcome) again joined me. We also involved many of the young children from Washington Temple to travel with us.

> *We were even called upon in the days to come to bury the dead!*

THE SOUL WINNER'S INSTITUTE

Prison and hospital ministry was only a part of what we were doing. Evangelist John D. Lawrence, the man of

God who had taught me soulwinning, after hearing about my dedication to the ministry, chose me to be the Vice President of The Soul Winner's Institute, and we (myself, he, his wife, and his children) traveled all over the United States, training people in many facets of soulwinning. What a privilege.

It's Not Us, But God

I urge all those who are ministering in any capacity to please remember that it's not you who's in charge; it's the power of the Holy Spirit. Don't ever lose your anointing by becoming slack, thinking you've got it made. The Lord will teach you to always stay in the realm of the anointing, and don't come out until you've completed the ministry. Then, you can praise the Lord, as you are leaving your place of ministry, being confident in this one thing, that your names are written in glory. We are just instruments in His hands.

We Are Fulfilling the Master's Commission

By ministering in the prisons, the hospitals, the streets, and wherever needy souls were to be found, we were fulfilling the Master's Commission for us here on earth. Jesus taught:

Then shall the King say unto them on his right hand, Come, ye blessed of my Father, inherit the kingdom prepared for you from the foundation of the world:

I HAVE CHOSEN YOU

for I was an hungered, and ye gave me meat: I was thirsty, and ye gave me drink: I was a stranger, and ye took me in: naked, and ye clothed me: I was sick, and ye visited me: I was in prison, and ye came unto me.

Then shall the righteous answer him, saying, Lord, when saw we thee an hungered, and fed thee? or thirsty, and gave thee drink? When saw we thee a stranger, and took thee in? or naked, and clothed thee? Or when saw we thee sick, or in prison, and came unto thee?

And the King shall answer and say unto them, Verily I say unto you, Inasmuch as ye have done it unto one of the least of these my brethren, ye have done it unto me.   Matthew 25:34-40

DON'T WAIT

I worked in the field for nearly twenty years without a missionary license, and never received any until I married Bishop Washington. That's why the Lord had given me John 15:16 that day on the train. He was telling me that He had ordained me Himself.

Many saints are saved and filled with the Holy Ghost, but they wait for their state bishop or supervisor to give them some papers. If those papers are not forthcoming, they do nothing. I want to challenge you today. Read the Word of God, and make your calling and election sure.

TRIED IN THE FIRE

Don't wait around, wasting your time and risking going into eternity without having obeyed the call of God. Suppose the Lord should come while you're reading this book. What excuse would you give Him for not having done what He has called all of us to do: preach the Gospel to every creature and bring souls into His Kingdom?

Chapter Eleven

I Have Put My Words in Your Mouth

Behold, I have put My words in your mouth.
See, I have appointed you this day over the nations
and over the kingdoms,
To pluck up and to break down,
To destroy and to overthrow,
To build and to plant.   Jeremiah 1:9-10, NAS

For a while, I actually thought that perhaps my work was completed. After all, I had accomplished ministry on the street, in the hospitals, in the nursing home, and in the prison. Then, the Lord enlightened my mind, and I began to understand that my work was just beginning.

Rikers Island

Now, the Lord opened a new door for us, with the

same group in Rikers Island Prison. They scheduled us for two services—the first from 7:30 to 8:30 in the morning.

When we entered the gymnasium, where the services were being held, I noticed that there was no piano. The leader of the group was talking with the officer, and the Lord said to me, "Go tell the officer to take the piano out of the closet." When I told him this, he responded as if I were crazy. I kept telling him, but he wouldn't listen. Shortly afterwards, the men started to gather for the service, so I left it at that.

Many Christian singers are accustomed to singing with a piano, and since there was no piano, one of the ladies started to sing off key. Young people are prone to express their feelings anywhere, and that day the young men started laughing right in the middle of the service. That deeply troubled me. They seemed to be just looking for something, anything, to keep them from being serious about their souls.

At the end of the service, they prepared a breakfast for us, but on the way to the dining hall, I told the group that I didn't intend to take one bite of food. We had just

> *We thanked God for honoring us and giving us a great harvest of souls!*

lost a large number of young men, who should have come to salvation. Instead, we were being laughed at, all because we didn't have a piano. We needed to repent for those souls, I told them, and go without food, to ask forgiveness from the Lord. Part of the group did give up the meal, and together we cried out to the Lord for forgiveness.

The next service began at nine o'clock, and we had a beautiful group of older men attending this one. The officer went into the closet and took out the piano, and we had church. Many souls came to Christ in that service, and we thanked God for honoring us and giving us a great harvest of souls.

Still, I left there complaining about how we must always operate God's ministry with a spirit of excellence. I was upset, but the Lord spoke to me and said, "If you don't like the way the leader is operating, leave him and go to the state." Based on that, I asked our ministry secretary, Vera Harrell, to make contact with the chaplain in upstate New York's infamous Sing-Sing Correctional and ask if we could come there to minister.

SING-SING

At the time, the chaplain at Sing-Sing was Richard K. Tanon, a powerful man of God, who had never had another group wanting to come in and minister. "What do you do?" he asked me.

"We sing, we give testimonies, and we deliver the Gospel," I told him.

"Okay," he said, "we'll give you an opportunity."

We started that ministry in 1968 and continued it even after Chaplain Tanon was transferred to Naponach Eastern Correctional Facility. He also invited us to minister there. We looked forward to that ministry each month, because many men received the Lord as their Savior. To our God be all the glory!

We Needed a Van for the Ministry

We had been putting lots of miles on our cars, and so we began praying that the Lord would bless us with a van. He granted our petition, and we were able to purchase a large maroon and white Dodge Ram van. We bought it empty, so that we could put our own custom-made seats inside. Nearly every seat in that van reclined, and I had my own captain's seat up front, beside the driver (when I wasn't driving myself).

That van was exactly what we needed to travel together, so that we could unite ourselves in prayer. We were mindful of the scriptural admonition that one could *"chase a thousand,"* but that two could *"put ten thousand to flight"* (Deuteronomy 32:30). When we traveled together, we experienced a greater level of power.

A Great Move of God at Sing-Sing

At Sing-Sing, we experienced some powerful moves of God. Once, the Lord laid it on my heart to pray for revival. While on my way through security one day, the Lord said, "Take your hat off, and put your robe on." That

I HAVE PUT MY WORDS IN YOUR MOUTH

Sunday morning, the Lord moved mightily. Rev. John McDonald brought the message, and the Lord told me to appeal to the men who had made a covenant with Him by sacrifice to come to the altar. There, we should have them repeat the sinner's prayer, and then we should anoint them with oil. The Lord would do the rest.

I have always been very sensitive about what I do in the presence of ordained ministers, so rather than do this myself, I asked Rev. McDonald to anoint the men with oil. But the Holy Ghost spoke and said, "I didn't tell *him* to anoint the men; I told *you*."

After repenting, I asked the Lord, "What do I do now?"

He said, "Lay your hands on every man who has the oil on his forehead, and I'll do the rest." As I laid my hands on them, the Holy Ghost hit them, and they were slain in the Spirit. We watched, as one by one, the men were filled with the power of God. What an experience it was to see those men begin to speak with other tongues. Before it was over, men were lying in the isles, drunk under the power of God.

Then the Lord said to me, "Anoint the chaplain." I laid my hands on him from behind, and he, too, began to speak in tongues under a powerful anointing. Then the other crusaders raised their hands to be anointed, and the Holy Ghost filled them again. The presence of God was awesome in that place.

BEDFORD HILLS

I asked the secretary to contact the chaplain at Bedford

Hills Women's Correctional Facility. This chaplain also responded favorably, and we ministered there for many years. In time, I asked him if we could do a two-day revival there, and he gave us permission.

The first evening of the meetings, the Spirit of God prepared the women, and on Sunday morning, during the regular service, one of the female officers started to speak in tongues. When this happened, the inmates went wild under the power of God, many of them also receiving the baptism of the Holy Ghost. We, too, received another filling.

The interesting thing was that the chaplain was Episcopalian, and, evidently, had never experienced a move of God like this before. He had a long beard that began to tremble, and I noticed that he seemed to be frightened. After the service that day, he told us to wait until he contacted us to come back the next time. Sadly, he never did contact us, but God had us do what He wanted that day, and we left there having obeyed the Lord.

Taconic

We also ministered in Taconic Men's Correctional Facility across the street from Bedford Hills. God blessed there too, and many men were saved.

Attica

I had a desire to visit with the men at Attica State Prison. I'd heard many things about that institution. The crusaders had now established a track record in the New

I HAVE PUT MY WORDS IN YOUR MOUTH

York State institutions, and when we contacted Chaplain Carter, asking if we could minister there, he immediately arranged for a visit once a year. We looked forward to going and decided that, since it was so far, we would trust God to let us fly there and stay overnight in a local hotel. We experienced beautiful fellowship at one of the finest restaurants in the area. Our visits to Attica usually happened in the month of October, and since a few of us were born in that month, we had some great birthday celebrations in that place.

EVERY INSTITUTION IN UPSTATE NEW YORK

We were determined to cover every correctional institution in upstate New York, and next we inquired about Elmira Correctional and reached the chaplain there. He, too, opened the doors to us. When we went there, it seemed as if the heavens had opened, and God began to touch the hearts of both inmates and officers of the institution. What a sweet, sweet spirit we experienced in that place!

> *We were determined to cover every correctional institution in upstate New York!*

We also visited Clinton, Danamora, and Comstock. God was very gracious to us, and we experienced His favor in each institution. I finally began to understand what God had been trying to say to me from Jeremiah:

See, I have this day set thee over the nations and over the kingdoms, to root out, and to pull down, and to destroy, and to throw down, to build, and to plant.

Jeremiah 1:10

We had been commissioned to take the Gospel, and it would root out sin, pull down strongholds, and destroy the works of the devil. As we went forth, sowing the Word of God into the hearts of men and women in the prisons around the state, God did His work. This, then, was our mandate from God.

THE CAROLINAS

Today, because my ministry is located in Charlotte, North Carolina, we minister here in prisons each second and third Sunday. On each fourth Sunday, we have similar meetings in South Carolina. I love the prison ministry, and God has blessed and anointed us for this service.

Chapter Twelve
Plenteous in Mercy

The Lord is merciful and gracious, slow to anger, and plenteous in mercy.   Psalm 103:8

After a time, the Lord laid it on my heart to attend Bible college. As a young person, my desire had been to teach school. I was never sure why or from where this ambition came, but in time, I became convinced that it was from the Lord.

Studying (and Teaching) Bible School

I enrolled in United Christian College in Brooklyn, New York, and was very excited about the systematic study of God's Word. The dean of the college evidently saw something in me, for after I had completed my studies in Christian Workers, Evangelism, General Bible 1, and General Bible 2, he asked me to teach Evangelism in the school. In one way, this was a surprise, and in another way, it was not. Soulwinning had long been my passion. I loved to win the lost, and I was sure that I could teach the subject by precept and by example.

I was living in Roosevelt, Long Island, at the time, and I drove to class every night. Pastor Raymond Cook, another professor at the college, usually rode with me. One night, after classes were over, Pastor Cook asked me if I could take him to the Veterans Administration Hospital located about forty miles away.

Visiting Elder William Connelly

At first, I thought to myself, "What nerve he has, asking me to take that long trip, when I need to get home to my girls!" But then he asked me again, and this time, he said something that got my attention. "Could you please drive me out to the hospital to see a dear friend of mine, Elder Connelly."

My friend Joan Robinson (now Joan McDonald) had told me about a wonderful pastor in Brooklyn, who had lost his wife the year before. His name was William Connelly. At the time, I wasn't interested. The last thing I wanted was another man. It had been only a year or so since I had buried my first husband, and I was just now breathing easy from that bad experience. Still, when I heard Pastor Cook say that name, Elder Connelly, I was somehow interested in taking that long drive.

When we got to the hospital, the room was dark, and only the light from a television set was visible. A lady could be seen seated in a chair next to Elder Connelly's bed. She had apparently just gotten off duty, because she was wearing a nurse's uniform. Strangely, even though I had never had any previous contact with this man, and had no reason to be jealous of another woman in his life, I somehow felt jealousy in that moment.

There was little time to ponder this strange phenomenon. After a few introductions, Pastor Cook said, "Let's pray," and we prayed for the healing of this man of God. When we were leaving, the young lady in the nurse's uniform left with us. I felt better, knowing that the two of them had not been left alone together. I couldn't wait to tell Joan about it, and we laughed together.

I was excited that God had allowed William and I to meet, but I promised myself that I would not go to the hospital to visit him again, for fear that

> *It had been only a year or so since I had buried my first husband, and I was just now breathing easy from that bad experience!*

other women would show up, and I would be embarrassed. Many people knew me now, because of the ministry I was doing in the church, and I didn't want rumors flying around that I was after a widower.

Don't Go To Work Today

A few days later, the Lord spoke to me and said, "Don't go to work today." I wondered what that could mean. Surely, the Lord wouldn't say such a thing. I hated to miss even one day of work. Still, I had been asking the Lord to teach me His voice, so that I would never follow the devil. Was this God? Or was it the enemy? I prayed that I would know for sure.

Then the Lord clearly gave me an assignment. I was to go to the hospital to visit Elder William Connelly, take him some cassettes with preaching on them and also take a portable tape player so that he could listen to the tapes.

I said, "Lord, You know I don't want to go there again. If I run into any church folk, they'll tell everyone that I was out running after Elder Connelly." But the Lord was not interested in my excuses; He just wanted me to be obedient.

I finally yielded to the command of the Lord, and when I got on the elevator to go up to William's room, there were about five women I knew riding up with me. One of them was his mother.

We all went in together, but I was surprised when Elder Connelly asked the others to wait outside, while he spoke with me privately. Then he did something very surprising. He looked deep into my eyes, and, smiling brightly, said, "Thank you for coming."

"I came to bring you some tapes of Bishop Washington's preaching," I said.

"That was kind," he answered, "but I don't have any way to play them here."

"I brought a tape player," I said and brought it out.

I was anxious to bring our conversation to a conclusion and leave him with the other "candidates." After I got out of there that day, I again promised myself that I would never go back to visit Elder Connelly. If the Lord wanted me to know when he came home from the hospital, He would have to let someone tell me.

His Ways Are Past Finding Out

A few nights later, I went to a diner on Linden Boulevard in Brooklyn. To my surprise, there was William's brother Ronald and his wife. We greeted each other, and then the very next words that came out of his mouth were these: "My brother William will be coming home from the hospital tomorrow." I couldn't help but conclude that God's ways are past finding out. How mighty our God is! He has a master plan for our lives, and He hadn't forgotten me.

Ronald's wife, without hesitation added, "I wouldn't mind having you for my new sister-in-law," and we both smiled.

I explained to Ronald that I had left a tape player belonging to our ministry group with his brother. Now

TRIED IN THE FIRE

that William was being released, I would need it back, I told him, so that we could pass it on to others in need. I suggested that someone leave it at their mother's house, since she lived close to the route I frequently had to travel.

When the time came, I took my daughter Pat with me and went to his mother's to get the tape player. She said it wasn't there. "William said for you to come to his house and get it," she said. That left me dismayed. I surely didn't want to go there.

I called the home and spoke with Elder Connelly's daughter Beverly. She said he wasn't home just then. I asked if she knew where the tape player was, and she said she did. "Could I come by and get it?" I asked. She said that would be fine.

I drove to the house and rang the door bell. Beverly answered the door and asked me to wait, while she brought the player. While I was waiting, her father drove up. What good timing! I wasn't ready for this.

I was very nervous, but I'm not sure it showed.

> *As we talked, looking into each other's eyes, I knew that it was love at first sight!*

PLENTEOUS IN MERCY

Elder Connelly greeted me and introduced me to his daughter. In turn, I introduced him to Pat. I felt very eager to cut things short and leave. He thanked me, and I rushed back to the car and drove off. Still, even as I drove away, I knew that I would be getting a phone call from him in the very near future. I was sure that God had arranged this little meeting.

A few days later, sure enough, I received the call inviting me to a dinner to discuss "some sort of investment." Elder Connelly picked me up and took me to a fabulous restaurant. As we talked, looking into each other's eyes, I knew that it was love at first sight.

We finished our entre and ordered dessert. As I was enjoying whatever it was that I had ordered, a strange thing happened: he began to feed me some of his cake. As he did this, all I could see was him feeding me a piece of our wedding cake. I knew that the future was evident. All thoughts of investments of every type were forgotten.

Just a few months later he asked the question, and I said yes, and we started making wedding plans.

A Home for Us

One of the first things William told me was that he wanted to buy us a house out on Long Island. By then, I already owned that small house. But *small* is the key word. It was like a doll house. We didn't have a shower, and if I didn't have oil in the tank, we didn't have hot water. I had been praying and asking the Lord to bless me with a shower, and He had showed me a vision of a shower that was yellow, black, and white.

I said "Lord, are You going to give me this?" And He said He would.

When Mama Fedie knew that we were looking for a house, she called to say that she had found just the right house for us. It was located on West Centennial Avenue in Roosevelt, New York. It was a five-bedroom brick colonial house with formal dining room, a living room, a large kitchen and kitchen nook, an additional space for an office, a half bath downstairs, and a full basement. All of this was sitting on nearly an acre of land, and it had a two-car garage.

The master bedroom was on the second floor, and I was amazed because it had it's own private shower. There were two other bedrooms and a very large (actually, huge) bathroom in the hall.

I walked into that hall bathroom, and immediately noticed that it was tiled in black, with a yellow sink, toilet, and bathtub. I wasn't sure it was the right place, for it didn't have exactly the color combination I had seen.

Then the Lord drew my attention to the colors in the wallpaper. It was white with gold running through it, and it was even more gorgeous than I had seen in the vision. This was the home the Lord had promised me.

Next, I entered the master bedroom, which covered the entire left side of the house. I opened another door, and there, in a private bathroom, was a beautiful blue-tiled shower. I was overwhelmed with emotion.

PLENTEOUS IN MERCY

"You asked Me for a shower," the Lord said, "and because of your faithful service to Me, I'm going to give you your own private shower, in addition to the beautiful one in the large bathroom in the downstairs hallway." It was all very wonderful.

WE NEEDED MY PASTOR'S BLESSING

We wanted to immediately put a contract on the house, and we wanted to set a date for the wedding, but first, we would need the blessing of Pastor Washington. In his church, I had been nurtured, taught, encouraged, and trained to win souls for Christ. I could not marry without his blessing. We made an appointment to see him at his earliest convenience.

Bishop questioned us, wanting to make sure this was what we both wanted to do, and then, without anything further, he gave us his blessings. With that, we were able to begin our planning in earnest.

A CHRISTMAS WEDDING

We placed a contract on the house, and we set the wedding date for December 8. It was to be a Christmas wedding, with all the beautiful colors and accents that would make it a most elegant affair. We reserved the dining hall at First Church of God in Christ, and I planned the kind of wedding I had been denied earlier in life.

Many were eager to be part of our wedding, and from them, I had to pick five bridesmaids, a maid of honor, two flower girls (I chose my grand nieces), and a ring bearer.

TRIED IN THE FIRE

I reserved one of the best photographers in New York, and a limousine, determined to make it all as grand as possible.

Since it was a Christmas wedding, the bridesmaids wore red gowns, with red and white bouquets, and the maid of honor wore green. All the men wore off-white tuxedos, with red cummerbunds and red and white boutonnieres. The best man wore a green boutonniere. The groom and I decided on off-white colors for ourselves too. We tried not to miss a thing in our planning. This was truly going to be the wedding of the century.

All was working well ... until I became too involved in the details and nearly forgot that I still had a ministry I must be faithful to.

Chapter Thirteen

Think It Not Strange

Beloved, think it not strange concerning the fiery trial which is to try you, as though some strange thing happened unto you: but rejoice, inasmuch as ye are partakers of Christ's sufferings; that, when his glory shall be revealed, ye may be glad also with exceeding joy.

1 Peter 4:12-13

It was Friday night, and I was supposed to be at Goldwater Hospital to do our regular Friday night service, but Mom Ivey had called to say that she was bringing over a man, whom she thought might be interested in purchasing my house. I should wait on them. That was good news. I had been praying for a buyer, and I was hoping that this was the answer to my prayers.

The girls and I hadn't eaten, and I was frying fish when Mom Ivey and the man arrived. Then one of the wedding party came by to get directions to the tuxedo rental store, and I had to take time to talk with him. I noticed that it was getting very late. What should I do?

I never missed the service at the hospital, but then I didn't have to plan a wedding every week or sell a house either. This was a special time in my life. Surely God wouldn't mind if I missed just this once, I reasoned.

> *Surely God wouldn't mind if I missed just this once, I reasoned!*

He knew that I was getting married, so everything else had to be put on hold. With that, I stopped worrying about the service and began concentrating on what was at hand.

Slipping on the Stairs

I had my living room and dining room sets upstairs on the second floor. The kitchen was so tiny that only a small table and two chairs fit into it. I said to Mom, "Let's go upstairs and eat," but she preferred eating downstairs, so I went upstairs to get a piano stool, so that I could join the two of them at the kitchen table. And, I suppose that I was hurrying.

Anyway, as I was coming back down the stairs, I slipped (the floor had some grease on it), and I went flying. The leg of the piano stool landed in the skillet of hot grease, and the hot grease splashed up on me.

THINK IT NOT STRANGE

It hit my forehead first and would have done immeasurable damage to my face, had it not been for the grace of God. He gave me wisdom to turn, and the hot grease, instead, went down my left arm and thigh. It was yet another experience of being tried in the fire, and this time, I experienced a fiery burning and a lot of terrible pain.

Mom and one of my daughters immediately started applying ice to my forehead. What they couldn't know was that hot grease was seeping through my clothes and causing third degree burns on other parts of my body. My other daughter ran outside to find an ambulance. The Lord, with His awesomeness, had placed a policeman across the street from the house, and he immediately dispatched an ambulance, which arrived within a very few minutes.

THE EMERGENCY WARD

When I got to the hospital, they bathed my burns in saline solution and bandaged them. Then they gave me instructions on how to continue this process every four hours for the foreseeable future, until the wounds were healed. This, they said, could well be a matter of life and death. If the burns became infected, I could die.

It was to be a very painful and frustrating process. Every time the contaminated gauze was removed, skin would come off with it. And the wounds looked absolutely terrible. How could I get ready for a wedding in this condition? And yet I must. I had no choice.

TRIED IN THE FIRE

WHY DID IT HAPPEN?

When all of this happened, some people wondered if the Lord was not trying to tell me something—like not to get married or not to marry this particular man. I didn't get that message at all. Then, why did it happen?

I had been so involved with the wedding plans that I had done something I had no right doing: putting my personal plans ahead of God's plans. I was concentrating on my wedding and, in the process, I was neglecting the ministry He had so graciously given to me.

I later reminded myself of the parable our Lord spoke:

> *A certain man made a great supper, and bade many: and sent his servant at supper time to say to them that were bidden, Come; for all things are now ready. And they all with one consent began to make excuse. The first said unto him, I have bought a piece of ground, and I must needs go and see it: I pray thee have me excused. And another said, I have bought five yoke of oxen, and I go to prove them: I pray thee have me excused. And another said, I have married a wife, and therefore I cannot come. So that servant came, and shewed his lord these things.*
> *Then the master of the house being angry said to his servant, Go out quickly into the streets and lanes of the city, and bring in hither the poor, and the maimed, and the halt, and the blind.*
> *And the servant said, Lord, it is done as thou hast commanded, and yet there is room.*

THINK IT NOT STRANGE

And the lord said unto the servant, Go out into the highways and hedges, and compel them to come in, that my house may be filled.   Luke 14:16-23

Our God is a jealous God, and we must remember to put Him first in every situation. As we noted in an earlier chapter, the Scriptures warn us against having any other gods before Him:

Thou shalt have no other gods before me.
Exodus 20:3

And that was exactly what was happening with me. I was putting getting married and planning the wedding above the ministry that God had entrusted to me. That spelled tragedy.

How I Got Through Those Days

It all happened the Friday after Thanksgiving, November 22, 1979, and the wedding was scheduled for sixteen days later. God sent two young ladies, Doris Brown and Hazel Alexander, who stayed with me through each night, bathing the burns and changing the bandages. What a sacrifice they made, not getting much sleep during those days, because this procedure had to be performed so often. Still, both of them went to work every morning.

As much as I was hurting, I still had to keep working on the wedding plans. When Mama Fedie saw me, she was very upset, thinking that I was rushing around too much and should be just taking it easy. But I simply had to complete the plans for the wedding. It was too important to neglect. It was now one week before the wedding, and almost everything was in place—except me.

I went back to the doctor, and when I told him that I was getting married in just a few days, he thought it was funny and had a good time laughing about it. He said that if he had known I had wedding plans so soon, he might have been able to do something. I didn't ask exactly what he could have done. Perhaps he meant using skin grafts. But apparently he thought it was too late for that now.

As the final days ticked off, and there was genuine excitement in the air, and yet I was still in excruciating pain. Elder Connelly remained calm and steadfast through this entire traumatic episode, and together, we were still trusting that all things were working together for our good. It would be a wonderful wedding, we were sure.

Our Wedding Day Dawns

On the morning of the wedding, snow began to fall, and trying to get into and out of the limousine in snow was not an easy thing. My maid of honor was near to tears, but we made it to Washington Temple, and there I climbed the stairs of the church and waited for the organ prelude to begin. This would be the signal for the wedding party to march in, before the groom preached his planned message: "Bone of my bone and flesh of my flesh."

Pop Morris was to escort me down the aisle, and he

THINK IT NOT STRANGE

kept asking me if I was sure I wanted to go through with the wedding. I assured him that I did and was listening for my queue, which was to be the words, "Lord, thank You for the woman, whom You have given me."

When I finally heard those words, I ascended the stairs, and there, before me, was a host of people, family, friends, and fellow believers, all present to witness our union before God. The church was full, and I managed a smile, as I looked forward to having someone to take care of me. The burns were still painful, but I was happy.

Bishop Washington married us, and he was elegant as always, knowing just how to put couples together "till death us do part." When he pronounced the words, "You may now salute the bride," the warm, sweet kiss and embrace of my bridegroom let me know that I was now in good hands. This man would assist God in helping me through the next few months of bathing the burns and changing the bandages, and his love would bring out the best in me for the future.

> *The groom preached his planned message: "Bone of my bone and flesh of my flesh!"*

TRIED IN THE FIRE

THE RECEPTION

We headed to the reception at First Church, and there we found the dining hall full of people and gifts. I clung to my husband, who had agreed to shield my left arm and hip from being too near those who greeted us so warmly. Those burns were too fresh and painful to inflict upon them any further damage.

THE ABORTED HONEYMOON

After a few hours, we escaped from the reception of our friends and well-wishers and headed for our honeymoon trip to Pennsylvania. We had reserved a suite with a heart-shaped Jacuzzi, and we looked forward to all the beautiful things newlyweds enjoy. But it was to be very different than we had imagined.

I was in such pain that I could not bear to be touched. Imagine it! Every time my very loving new husband touched me, I would scream out in pain. He ended up driving me back to Long Island to the hospital, and the doctor there scheduled me for a skin graft operation.

This was a very serious procedure, and since the risk of infection was great, everyone who visited me had to fully cover themselves in hospital gowns, shoe coverings, and head covering and scrub in. Everything in the burn unit had to be sterile, so that no infection would occur. In a surgical procedure, they took skin from my thigh and, with it, covered my arm and hip.

Being seriously burned is a traumatic experience, one that I would not wish upon my worst enemy—even if I had one. I lost many months of work, and it was almost a year before I felt total relief from the pain of it.

OTHER SERIOUS ADJUSTMENTS

There were other serious adjustments. It took William's daughters, Eileen and Beverly, months before they could get used to having a stepmother in their life. I remember one of them saying to me one day early on, "You're not my mother." I gently reminded them that I was the woman their father had chosen, and assured them they would eventually get used to that fact. But, like the healing of the burns, it was a very slow process.

In the days ahead, one of them put a photo of their mother in her casket inside the dirty clothes basket, where I would find it. They insisted that their dad take them to the cemetery every few days to visit their mother's grave.

In time, the girls chose to call me, Mumzie. The name caught on, and many of the young people of the church called me by that name. Three who were young people at that time—Bonnie Snead (one of my babies, married now and living in Connecticut), Eddie Connelly (William's nephew), and Eddie Harris—still call me that today.

When I visited with Eddie Harris and his beautiful wife Michelle in Houston, Texas, not long ago, his children called me Mumzie. "Don't call her that," their father protested.

"Then, what should we call her?" they asked.

He thought a minute, and then replied: "Grand-Mumzie." I thought it was the cutest name I'd ever been called.

The members of Elder Connelly's congregation, Mt. Sinai Church of God in Christ #2, or Mt. Sinai #2, as we all called it, also had a very difficult time accepting me. It was a family church, and many members of his family worshiped and officiated there. So, if it wasn't enough adjusting to a new husband, a new home and a new life, I had the challenge of my wounds, my new stepdaughters, and my adopted church family. It took a lot of prayer to get through that.

ELDER CONNELLY WAS A DELIGHT

As for Elder Connelly himself, he was a pure delight. He was an excellent cook and a dedicated husband. He studied books on how to properly care for a wife, and he applied what he learned in them to take good care of me. He even made sure I had no uncared-for corns on my toes.

> *He studied books on how to properly care for a wife, and he applied what he learned in them to take good care of me!*

THINK IT NOT STRANGE

I had been very thankful for the ladies who had cared for me in those early days of my suffering, but having a companion to wake up and change my bandages at all hours of the night was so much better. The ladies had to leave me every morning and go to work, but my husband was not working a secular job, and so he was available day and night. It was because of William's loving care that I healed in record time.

This is made all the more wonderful when we realize that William Connelly was not a well man himself. A Veteran of the Vietnam War, he had developed sickle cell anemia. This is what had placed him in the hospital, where I first met him. The Lord had touched him, but the sickness came back. After we were married, he was never well enough to return to his day job. That's what made him available to me. And our life together was delightful. That's what made it hard to leave him when the time came.

Invited To Minister in Ghana

Not long after I had fully recovered from this trauma, a minister of the Gospel, Rev. David Smith, called one day to say that the Lord had told him to take a group to Ghana, Africa, to minister, and he wanted me to go along. I had a problem with that. I had been married only a short time, and most of the time we had been together I had been in pain. Now that my husband had nursed me back to health, should I agree to leave him? He was not well enough to travel to Ghana. I didn't think so. I just told the brother that I didn't have the money to go and left it at that.

TRIED IN THE FIRE

This was true. Since William had not been working, our bills had piled up, and we were even in serious danger of losing our lovely home. That was another reason I hated to leave him. He was very willing for me to go, but how it would happen was another question entirely.

I was still acting as volunteer chaplain for Goldwater Hospital, and I mentioned in my meeting there one night the fact that someone had felt led to invite me to go to Ghana with them. I laughed and said that it would take a miracle from God to send me. One of the men at the hospital told me to see him the next week, and, when I did, he gave me a hundred dollar bill. That was the first seed sown into my life for that trip. In the coming days, more than two thousand dollars was received, and I was off to Ghana. Alas, I had to leave my bridegroom at home praying, while I helped to take the Gospel to desperate men and women in that newly-independent African nation.

Favor in Ghana

Rev. Smith had booked hotel rooms for us in Ghana, but after we entered the country, the Lord gave us favor with the people. The minister of Cafordra Province let a group of us stay in his guest house. He also made his servants available for our meals. We ministered in the railroad station, in the market place, and in the city streets, and many souls were brought to the saving knowledge of Christ. We learned to sing with the people in their language, and how they loved the Lord!

THINK IT NOT STRANGE

The average life span of the people of Ghana was only forty-seven years. Because of their poverty, they had no refrigerators and had to salt their food to preserve it and keep it from spoiling. The nation had just gained its independence from Britain, and they didn't yet have the tools and machinery needed to process the gold and other resources that could eventually give them financial security. We prayed over that country, and later we heard of many miracles that God did. That trip was one of the highlights of my life.

HEALING FOR THE DISEASE OF POVERTY

One day, after we had ministered and had the altar call, someone called for all those who were sick to come forth for prayer. Then the interpreter said, "All of you come to the altar, because you're *all* sick. You're poor, and poverty is a sickness, for which we need healing." That touched me very deeply.

We had been told in advance not to expect offerings. The people of Ghana, we were told, had not yet learned to sow into the lives of those who ministered to them. We were pleasantly surprised to find that some begged to give us their offerings. They said, "Let us give, because if we sow out of our small substance, we can reap great blessings from God." We had no choice but to give them the opportunity to share in the offerings.

Today, the people of Ghana have the tools and machinery to process their natural resources, and they are able to export to other countries and also to import the goods they need in return. What a blessing! God uses ordinary people to take this life-changing Gospel to the world.

OVERNIGHTING IN FRANCE

We had worked diligently in Ghana, and when we left, we were to spend a night in France, before returning home. We boarded the plane in Ghana and spent the night in France, but as we were taking off from there the next day, the plane suffered some sort of engine trouble. We disembarked and eventually were told that we would have to wait until the next day to fly.

God works in mysterious ways His wonders to perform. I'm not sure what I might have picked up in Ghana, but I was feeling very sick that day, as we were attempting to take off from France. My temperature was high, and I had diarrhea. I hadn't told anyone, because I figured that once we got airborne, I would be all right. But the flying time to the U.S. was nine hours or more, and that would have been a long time to spend in the air while I was feeling so badly. I always believed that the Lord had that plane malfunction just for me, so that I could get better before flying.

GOD HADN'T FORGOTTEN ME

They finally assigned us to our rooms for the night, and I was happy to get into bed. Still, it was a torment lying there, not knowing whether what I had might be a life-threatening sickness, such as malaria.

THINK IT NOT STRANGE

There was a young man on that trip whom I had claimed for my son. He was Antonio Mims. Just then, Antonio knocked on my door. He said, "Mom, the Lord sent me in here to pray for you." You can just imagine how happy I was to know that God was concerned about me. Antonio prayed, and a miracle immediately took place. I was healed.

In the middle of the night, I called home and spoke with William, sharing with him this wonderful testimony. Hearing his voice made me even more anxious to get back home to him. After all, we were still on our honeymoon.

> *I always believed that the Lord had that plane malfunction just for me!*

CAUGHT IN AN AIR TRAFFIC CONTROL STRIKE

The next day, to our amazement, we were told that we were in the midst of an air traffic control strike. Why was this happening? I thought I knew.

The Lord knew that I didn't need to make that long trip back to the US just then, as much as I was missing my wonderful husband. I needed time to recuperate my strength. My boss would not have understood if I had just gotten back from a twenty-one-day trip overseas and then immediately taken sick leave. So God had it all under control.

We were flown to London and put up in a fine hotel, where we were given three lovely meals a day. This all seemed to be God's bonus to us for our labor of love in Ghana.

The airlines contacted our employers to let them know what was happening, and by the time I got back to my husband and to my work at IBM, I was not only healed; I was also rested.

Sacrifice

Going on that trip and leaving my husband at home was a great sacrifice. Sometimes, I still feel the Lord asking us, as He did Simon Peter:

> *Lovest thou me more than these?* John 21:15

What He means by this is: are we so caught up in relationships, or jobs, or anything else that we can't give Him first place in our lives? I loved my husband and didn't want to leave him to go anywhere, but God called me, and I had to surrender my all to Him. He is the One who really matters. Jesus said that if we love Him, we'll keep His commandments (John 14:15). Obedience, His Word teaches us, is *"better than sacrifice"*:

> *And Samuel said, Hath the L*ORD *as great delight in burnt offerings and sacrifices, as in obeying the voice*

THINK IT NOT STRANGE

of the LORD*? Behold, to obey is better than sacrifice, and to hearken than the fat of rams.* 1 Samuel 15:22

ELDER CONNELLY'S DEPARTURE

Elder Connelly and I were able to do many things together, but our time to do it was tragically short. After just a year and eleven months of our life together, he checked out of this life and left me alone again. I could just imagine him resting comfortably in Heaven, without a care. He had loved me well, and now He deserved Heaven.

We gave him a well-deserved home-going, but the memory of this very sweet man of God lingers on.

Chapter Fourteen

The Lord Your God Is with You

*Only be strong and very courageous; be careful to do according to all the law which Moses My servant commanded you; do not turn from it to the right or to the left, so that you may have success wherever you go. This book of the law shall not depart from your mouth, but you shall meditate on it day and night, so that you may be careful to do according to all that is written in it; for then you will make your way prosperous, and then you will have success. Have I not commanded you? Be strong and courageous! Do not tremble or be dismayed, for the L*ord *your God is with you wherever you go.* Joshua 1:7-9, NAS

Not long after Elder Connelly went to his reward, I was speaking with Bishop Washington on the phone one day, and he asked me to pray with him, because he needed a leader for his youth department. I told him that I would pray and asked if he had anyone in mind. He said he did. I was that person.

STAYING AT MT. SINAI #2 FOR A YEAR

For this and other reasons, I really wanted to go immediately back to Washington Temple, but after praying about it, I was led to stay at Mt. Sinai #2 for a year. I needed to spend some more time with those people and to get the victory over all the things I'd been going through there.

I'd like to encourage anyone who wants to leave a church because of some situations you've experienced there to make sure to seek the Lord and get the victory, before going on to another church. That pleases the Lord. Eventually, the Lord released me, and I returned to my home church.

BACK HOME AT WASHINGTON TEMPLE

That first Sunday I was back home, I went to the altar to renew my vows to God and my membership to the church. Mom Washington said to me, "You didn't have to come back to the altar. You were honorably married to a pastor, and you had to go with him." I had just wanted to do everything right, for I wanted the Lord to be pleased with my life.

Bishop Washington did appoint me as his youth leader, and I had a beautiful group of young people, who loved God and wanted to be what He had called them to be. We

THE LORD YOUR GOD IS WITH YOU

spent many nights together in fasting and tarrying before the Lord. As a result, those were (and still are) some powerful young people. Today, they are operating in the fivefold ministry: apostles, prophets, evangelists, pastors, and teachers.

BISHOP WASHINGTON'S ELEVATION

When Bishop O.M. Kelly went home to be with the Lord, Bishop Washington, who had been serving as his assistant, was now installed as Jurisdictional Prelate over the Eastern New York Diocese. There was a lot of excitement around the state, and a group of us, Dr. Faye Ellis Butler, Chaplain Barbara Williams, and myself, became prayer partners for Bishop and Madam Washington and their family. Dr. John Lawrence and his wife Ethel lent prayer support also.

> *I wanted the Lord to be pleased with my life!*

Together, we were led of the Lord to go on a three-day fast and seek His face for victories in the lives of our new leaders, and it was agreed that we should invite Bishop Washington to join us at a retreat site in upstate New York for this purpose. He was an extremely busy man (with a very sick wife), and he probably would not have accepted this invitation—if we had not insisted that he could rest AND FISH. Fish seemed to be the magic word that got him there. He loved to fish.

In the end, we were unable to get reservations at the place we had intended to stay (the place that had fishing), and we had to settle on a Christian resort. This proved to be the will of God for many reasons.

I was blessed to be able to attend this gathering, only because I was out of work on sick leave. I would have to leave for a while the next day and keep a doctor's appointment in the city, an hour or two away, but then I would be back. The others felt that they needed to pray personally with Bishop Washington that morning, and I told him before I rushed off to my appointment.

I really hated to leave, and I prayed as I traveled. This was an important event. But, with Dr. and Mrs. Lawrence, Dr. Faye and Chaplain Barbara there, I could leave, and they would minister in the glory of God. We were all convinced that Bishop would never be the same after he had come to that retreat site.

When I returned from the doctor's appointment, I saw Dr. John Lawrence with his arms around Bishop Washington, praying for him under a powerful anointing. He seemed to be shaking him, and I knew that it was a mighty visitation of the Holy Ghost and fire. I never knew exactly what transpired that day, but I sensed that Dr. John Lawrence was somehow putting his life on the line for Bishop Washington. Amazingly, Dr. Lawrence became seriously ill not many days after that and went home to be with the Lord.

THE LORD YOUR GOD IS WITH YOU

A New Anointing

When I went back to the city, Bishop Washington had a speaking engagement at Bishop Huey Rogers' church. The place was full on a weeknight, and Bishop Roy Brown was there. Everyone sat in awe, as the Holy Ghost used Bishop in a way that none of us had ever seen him used before. Souls were saved, delivered, set free, and made whole that night. God had sent revival into his life, and everybody around him was feeling the effects.

The prayer team also asked permission to go to the Washington home and pray with Madam Washington, and we received approval from her and her family to do that. Together, we lay on our faces before God, weeping and seeking God for her healing. We left, trusting that our request had been granted.

Then the Lord spoke to me the next day and said that He was not going to heal Sister Washington. She was tired of battling her sickness and had given up on life, so He would not be able to leave her in this world much longer. Within a few days, while I was in Memphis at a class reunion, I received news from one of the saints in New York that Mom Washington had gone to be with the Lord.

I got back home in time for the home-going service, a well-deserved celebration for a mighty and faithful woman of God. I was on the program, to represent the youth department, and when it was time for me to speak, I noticed that Bishop Roy Brown was saying something to Bishop Washington. He put things on hold until I had finished my remarks.

TRIED IN THE FIRE

One of the things I remember saying that day was that we were committed to taking good care of the Bishop. When he heard that, he sort of shook his head, as if to say, "I'm going to hold you to that."

ALREADY KILLED TWO HUSBANDS

Three of us on the prayer team had lunch with Bishop Washington during the Spring Conference. That night, during the night session, he told everyone that he had eaten lunch with three lovely ladies. One of them, he said, had already killed two husbands. "Let me stay away from her," he joked. Everyone laughed at that line, but to me, it wasn't funny. I was the lady in question, and only I knew what it was to experience the death of two husbands.

> *Only I knew what it was to experience the death of two husbands!*

What he said that day surprised me for another reason. I hadn't known that he was interested. He had never been fresh with me, had never made a pass at me, and he had given me no clue to the fact that I was ever on his mind. I called him the next day and complained. "Dad," I said, "you embarrassed me in front of all those people last night, saying that I had already killed two husbands and you wanted to stay away from me. I didn't know you were interested."

Then I concluded, "Well, I just want you to know that they died happy." And, with that, I hung up the phone.

Not long afterward, one of his friends told me that I should stop calling him dad. It seems that he was interested in me being more than a daughter to him. I pondered this in my heart and began to pray for the will of the Lord to be done in this situation.

One day I went into Bishop's office to confirm a date for some youth activity, and as I was walking out the door, he grabbed me and gave me a kiss I would never forget. I left that day speaking in tongues. I went all the way to the secretary's office to confirm the date for the youth activity, and both she and I spoke in tongues. That was enough of a sign to let me know that Jesus was somewhere in the plan.

Before long, Bishop proposed to me, saying that he, too, wanted to die happy. But did this make any sense? This man was more than twenty-six years my senior. He was seventy-two, and I was just forty-seven at the time. You can imagine that I did a lot of praying, and in the end, I decided that this was the will of God, and I would yield to it.

THE NEED FOR SECRECY

Neither Bishop nor I believed in courtship at our age, so very soon after he expressed his interest in me, we started procedures to get married. But we had to do everything secretly, and that was very difficult.

Why the secrecy? There were two main reasons. (1) His wife had passed away just ten months before, and the tradition in the church was to wait a year before remarrying. (2) He was so new to his office that he was afraid to rock the boat, for fear he would anger someone and lose what he had spent many years gaining.

I understood all that, but that didn't make it any easier.

We went to my doctor in Brooklyn to get our blood tests. But, before we went that day, I called the doctor to explain that we didn't want to come in and be seated in the waiting room, for fear that someone who knew us might see us there, and begin spreading rumors before we were ready to make an official announcement. The doctor cooperated with us, and we went immediately to a back room, where we were attended to. Then, we eagerly awaited the results of the blood tests, so that we could tie the knot.

The next day, we went to the Jersey City Court House to apply for our marriage license, and we spoke with Bishop Chandler D. Owens, whom we wanted to perform the ceremony. We were married a few days later and took off for a short honeymoon.

The Agony of Secrecy

The worst part about being secretly married was that we had to sneak around to see each other. I didn't feel very comfortable with this, and yet we had to go through some really sneaky situations.

THE LORD YOUR GOD IS WITH YOU

We had gotten married at the end of June, and the UNAC (the United National Auxiliary Convention) was held, as usual, in July. There, the Bishop was ensconced in a gorgeous room in an exquisite hotel, and I had to stay at a little dumpy place, because I hadn't preregistered. After spending the first night with him and being told that I had to leave before daylight, so that no one would see me, I said to myself, "But he's my husband."

That didn't matter, so I would have to wait for the sign that it was safe for me to meet him again. It didn't come during the convention. Thank God, the convention lasted less than a week.

The challenges kept coming. Two months passed, and we still couldn't announce our marriage.

Several people were unkind to me during this time, but there was one man in particular, who just hated me. The Jurisdiction had appointed me editor of their newsletter, and I chose to sit in the lobby of the church and distribute the latest copies as the people entered. To do this, I needed a small table and a chair, and I called my husband, and asked him to send them. I never imagined that he would send them out with this particular man.

When he got there, he was obviously angry and asked me, "How did you have the nerve to ask Bishop to send you this chair? I should beat you all over this lobby."

That made me angry, and I said, "You and what army?"

He continued to harass me for months after that, making signs over my head in public, pretending to tilt the fan over on me as I marched around to give my offering, breathing out continuous threats every time I went to church. I just kept praying and trusting that one day God would avenge me of this adversary.

Someone told Bishop Roy Brown about the many things that were going on, and he called Bishop Washington and told him about it. When he asked me why I hadn't told him, I explained that I hadn't wanted to worry him, because he had the local, state, and national church on his shoulders, and I could pray and God would fix it. Also, if I had told him and he had spoken to the man, it just might have made things worse. I had chosen, instead, to just tell Jesus, and was sure that He would repair the situation in time.

This man hated me long after my husband had passed away. Then, one day, Elder Timothy Wright, the famous Gospel artist, went into an apartment building across the street from the church and found him lying there on the floor, dying from AIDS. He picked him up and carried him to the hospital.

He was later asked if he wanted someone to send for me, so that he could apologize to me, but he said no. I prayed many days for him. We're all God's children, and He loves us each one. Still, what he did was a dangerous thing. God has warned:

He permitted no man to oppress them,
And He reproved kings for their sakes, saying,
"Do not touch My anointed ones,
And do My prophets no harm."
                                        1 Chronicles 16:21-22, NAS

THE LORD YOUR GOD IS WITH YOU

We must be very careful how we treat each other, because one day we will give an account to God.

FACING A DIFFICULT CHOICE

Well, I kept going through. One day, a very handsome fellow came by my house during the Christmas holidays. He was the widower of a friend of ours, and he had often ministered with us whenever he was in town. When his wife died, he paid off our van, feeling that his wife, having been dedicated to the ministry, would want to leave something behind in her memory. Later, as we were traveling to the prison together, he broke down and said, "Gwen, I'm madly in love with you."

I didn't know what to say. He was a wonderful, anointed man, and I was sure that he would make a wonderful husband, but I already had a husband. That, however, I could *not* say. So what could I say? I told him to take his time and let the Lord give him direction. There was no rush for him to remarry. But he saw things another way. Later in the holidays, when we were alone for a moment, he said, "Gwen, will you marry me?"

TRIED IN THE FIRE

It is difficult to describe my feelings in that moment. I knew that I was already married, but since we hadn't yet announced it (and I wasn't sure when we could), I was thinking that perhaps I could get an annulment. Spending the rest of my life with this forty-five year old handsome man of God was a very appealing thought.

We went to sunrise service that Christmas, and Bishop Washington said, "Here comes a young man who has just recently buried his wife, and now he's back in New York to find himself another one."

"Yes," I said to myself, "he's after *your* wife."

What could I say? The man was a very anointed preacher, and he loved God. Bishop and I had been secretly married now for six months, and I was ready to give up the idea of ever having a peaceful marriage with him. I told him this one night, and he called Bishop Owens and said, "Chandler, I've simply got to announce this marriage."

They decided that the announcement should be made at a banquet always held after the election. In that election, Bishop Washington was elected as Second Vice Assistant Bishop of the Churches of God in Christ, Inc. and also reelected to the General Board. There our "intentions" were made known.

Bishop J.O. Patterson took us through the wedding vows again (as if we had never done it the first time), and our marriage finally became public knowledge in February of 1985. It was almost a year after we had first been joined in marriage.

THE LORD YOUR GOD IS WITH YOU

How did I bear all that? The Bible says:

He giveth power to the faint; and to them that have no might he increaseth strength. Even the youths shall faint and be weary, and the young men shall utterly fall: but they that wait upon the LORD *shall renew their strength; they shall mount up with wings as eagles; they shall run, and not be weary; and they shall walk, and not faint.*   Isaiah 40:29-31

In my own strength, I had wanted to throw in the towel, but I knew deep down inside of me that I had a charge to keep and a God to glorify. When we are called by God, it's not all peaches and cream, but we must trust and obey.

THE HONEYMOON

When I was finally free to do it, I told the younger man about our wedding, and he flew from California to be with us during the celebration. He took it all very hard, but he was gracious enough to reserve a beautiful suite in a fabulous hotel in San Francisco for Bishop and me as a wedding gift. We went there on our way to the honeymoon in Hawaii.

We traveled first class every step of the way. When we reached Hawaii, the saints there met us at the airport, with lots of gifts, and took us by their church, where Bishop preached, and we shared wonderful fellowship with them, before retiring to our hotel.

TRIED IN THE FIRE

After a few days in Hawaii, we went on to New Orleans for a few more days, and then to New Mexico for a week. It was the month of February, when the church always gave Bishop a full month of vacation.

Needless to say, there were a few unhappy people because of me being Bishop Washington's choice, but we survived their unhappiness. I was determined to be the wife he needed.

> *In the days to come, I spent much time in prayer!*

BEING USED OF GOD

In the days to come, I spent much time in prayer, and the Lord gave me Mother Elsie Shaw as a mentor. She spent a lot of time in our home, and wonderful nuggets of truth were sown into my life from this mighty woman of God. She was a shield and protector that God used in my life, to keep me focused and encouraged. I loved that mighty prophetess, prayer warrior, and gorgeous woman of God. She didn't like to be called mother, but preferred to be called simply Evangelist Elsie Shaw.

Then, one day, Mother Wallace asked me if I would like to speak for the Women's Day during the Spring Conference. I agreed. Mother Shaw flew in from Dayton, Ohio, to be with me, as I turned my plate down for a few

THE LORD YOUR GOD IS WITH YOU

days, and lay before the Lord, seeking His favor and His empowerment to deliver the message for the people.

The subject I chose for the occasion was: "The Legacy of Peace." A legacy is a law, it's money or property left by someone in a will, or it's something that is handed down from an ancestor or predecessor. I was thinking of the many times I had been tried in the fire. Before I married Bishop Washington, there was one kind of fire, but now there was a very different kind of heat. I had every right to choose this subject, for experience is always the best teacher.

As I ministered that day, I could hear my husband in the background, amazed at how God was using me. He was known as a prince of preachers, and both he and Bishop Ithiel Clemmons were in shock that day, mighty men of God that they were. Bishop Clemmons, who was the assistant to my husband, was the speaker for the next night. When he stood, he said, "After Sister Washington spoke last night, where can I go?" That was a great compliment, because God had always given him a powerful word.

When it came his turn, Bishop Washington commented, "My wife really gave an account for herself today." It was all God's doing.

I had many engagements after that night. I think I was the Women's Day speaker for almost every church in the Jurisdiction. I would have both morning and afternoon appointments, and I give the glory to Jesus.

TRIED IN THE FIRE

My Years with Bishop Washington

My years spent with Bishop Washington were a wonderful time of traveling, meeting people, and hearing him preach a powerful Gospel that caused many souls to be born into the Kingdom. What a crown he'll wear someday!

Then he suffered a serious stroke. At his bedside, one of his superintendents said to me, "Let him go. He doesn't want to live any longer."

"I can't give up my husband that easily," I protested.

Eventually, God made that decision for us and took him.

Job Well Done

After Bishop's death, the Lord spoke to me and said, "Job well done!" What a word that was, letting me know that this had been more of a ministry than a marriage. I had done what the Lord led me to do, and I was glad for it.

I had taken good care of the Bishop, feeding him the best foods: steaks that melted in his mouth, fresh vegetables, not frozen or canned. I decorated his home with the colors of the General Board—purple and white. The drapes, bedspread, and carpet, were plush and beautiful, so that he could live out his days in luxury. The house, throughout, indicated that a very special mighty man of God resided there. I had someone living in to help keep the house neat and clean, so that I could spend time traveling with and looking after the man himself.

THE LORD YOUR GOD IS WITH YOU

Before he preached his final sermon (at the Memphis Convocation), he told the people that he was happier than he'd ever been in his life. I had done my best, and I thank God for the opportunity.

God Is My Source

I was surprised to learn, shortly before the Bishop's death, that, because of the circumstances of our marriage, the church would do nothing for me after my husband was gone. This was devastating. Early in our marriage, I had asked the Lord to touch Bishop's heart to make some provision for me. In that moment, the Lord spoke to me and said, "I am your Source."

That didn't seem quite right to me. I was now the wife of a powerful bishop of the church, and I expected to look to him for my guidance and my provision in the days ahead. So, I didn't quite understand what the Lord was trying to show me. Then, after my husband had died, the Lord said, "Where is your source now?"

"I guess in the grave," I had to answer.

"He wasn't your source then, and he cannot be now," the Lord said. "But since I'm your Source, I'll take good care of you." And God has kept His Word. He is still taking good care of me.

I never saw the benefits of an insurance policy. If Bishop had one, I was not the recipient. The church voted to sell his house (which had been deeded to the organization), and his children, Fredrika and Ernest, received a share of the sale. I received nothing.

Worst of all, there was no will. Men and women of God, make out a will and designate where your money should go, if and when you should die. Don't sit by and let the State dictate how your legacy will be divided or force your family and friends into probate court to decide things—because you failed to take care of business. You owe it to your spouse and children to do the right thing for them.

Why worry about what they will do after you die? Why should you care? You made a vow, and that vow was "till death us do part." Don't worry about what they'll do after death. Your link to them ends there. Let go, and let God direct them as to what's next for their life. If you love them, you want them to be happy *all* the days of their lives. So, don't make things any more difficult for them in the future. Take care of that part of things, so that they won't have to rely on the charity of the church, or the next pastor and his wife, to meet their basic needs. This is only right, and God expects you to make right decisions.

YOU HAVE SOMETHING VERY POWERFUL

Bishops, superintendents, pastors, and minister's wives, seek the Lord in fasting and prayer. You have something so very powerful inside of you. He is the Holy Ghost, and when He lives in us, He will be a well of water, springing up. As we noted in an earlier chapter He promised that our gift would make room for us and

THE LORD YOUR GOD IS WITH YOU

bring us before great men, and I'm a witness to the truth of that promise. You may not yet know what's on the inside of you. But God's promise to you is:

> *Ask, and it shall be given you; seek, and ye shall find; knock and it shall be opened unto you.*   Matthew 7:7

Don't expect your life to be easy. The higher your position in ministry, the more trials you will experience. Nevertheless, do as Paul admonished the church:

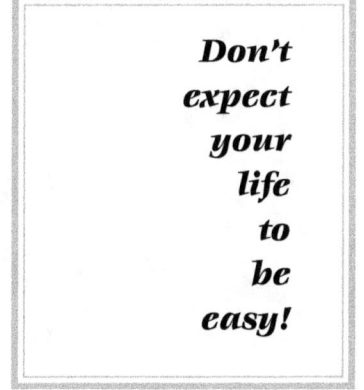

Don't expect your life to be easy!

> *Let the peace of God rule in your hearts.*
> Colossians 3:15

Never allow the trials of this world to cause you to be shut down with cancer, heart disease, high blood pressure, diabetes, or any other sickness caused by worry, stress, or unrest.

Peace is a heavenly word, and you can have perfect peace. When, at the advent of our Lord, angels came to sing among men a midnight sonnet, their second note was this:

> *On earth peace.*   Luke 2:14

TRIED IN THE FIRE

And, just as peace was declared at His birth, Jesus also left us with a good word about peace before He departed:

Peace I leave with you; My peace I give to you; not as the world gives, do I give to you. Do not let your heart be troubled, nor let it be fearful.   John 14:27, NAS

Always know who you are and Whose you are.

Chapter Fifteen

God Is Not Unrighteous to Forget Your Work

For God is not unrighteous to forget your work and labour of love, which ye have shewed toward his name, in that ye have ministered to the saints, and do minister.

Hebrews 6:10

After the death of Bishop Washington, I knew that things would change dramatically for me at Washington Temple. After all, I was no longer the First Lady of the church. It did not seem appropriate for me to stay there. But where should I go?.

My Next Move?

Patricia had lived for a while with my sister Carol in Charlotte, North Carolina, and she liked it so much that she wanted to move there. It was a beautiful city, and the rents were cheap. I visited Charlotte and found a nice house for rent there, the church paid my moving expenses, and that way one moving van moved both our things.

In one way, it was heartbreaking, leaving New York and relocating elsewhere. I loved New York, and I still do. It was the place where both of my daughters were born and raised, the place of my spiritual birth and growth, the place of many joyous experiences (and, also, of some sad times). I have always said that New York is the city to spend Christmas and New Years Holidays in, and, for the past nineteen years, that's what it has become for me. But New York is no longer my home.

> *The church paid my moving expenses, and I was suddenly back in the South I loved!*

Adjusting to My New Home

I found a job with a Charlotte travel agency and began to look around to see which of the churches I wanted to join. There were only a few of our churches there. One of those churches was being pastored by a lady, someone I knew. She was Missionary Pastor Lillie Austin (now deceased). Sister Austin had

GOD IS NOT UNRIGHTEOUS TO FORGET YOUR WORK

also moved to Charlotte from New York, and when she asked me if I would come and work with her at Pilgrim Assemblies, I couldn't say no. After all, when I had needed workers for the prison ministry in New York, she had come and brought some fifty missionaries from her church, both men and women.

I joined the ministry and began going door-to-door, witnessing and gleaning a harvest of children for Sunday school. I knew that if the parents let their children come, we would soon have the parents too. I worked with her in this way for several years.

Then I became homesick for the Church of God in Christ. I was a second-generation member, and I loved this grand old church, but I realized that I should wait on the Lord for His direction.

For a time, I did conduct services in my living room. One family after another joined us, until we were forced to move our services to the Ramada Inn and, from there, to an even larger space. But I was not called to pastor. My work was in evangelism, winning souls for the Kingdom.

After I married Bishop Washington, I had resigned most of my posts, to give my full time to caring for him, but now I realized that soulwinning would always be my first love. I began doing volunteer work around the community, the prisons, the schools, and the rest homes.

FINDING THE RIGHT CHURCH

Mother Elsie Shaw told me she felt that I should join Bishop Leroy Jackson Woolard's Jurisdiction in North

Carolina, and I heard that he was coming to town to install a new pastor. I thought I knew who it would be.

I had met a dear man of God and his wife, through my daughter Patricia, because she went to see a house they had up for sale. He was Superintendent Tommie Murphy. When I met him, he shared with me that his pastor, Superintendent E.C. Cannon, had passed away, and he was carrying the ministry, until a new pastor was chosen. I knew in that moment that *he* would be that new pastor, so I went there to witness the installation and to hear Bishop Woolard speak. After hearing the choir and feeling the warmth of the members, I decided that I wanted to be a part of the ministry at New Bethel Church of God in Christ.

In time, Pastor invited me speak, and I joined under watch care and began to set up the new member's class with Missionary Cynthia Cannon, the daughter of the founder. I love the ministry and the people at my church, and I know that they lift me up in prayer when I am absent and in some other ministry endeavor.

WE ARE ALL CALLED TO SOULWINNING

After I married Bishop Washington, I somehow got the idea that I had spiritually outgrown witnessing on the streets, passing out tracts, and going to the prisons to win souls. Before leaving New York, as the widow of Bishop Washington, I was again teaching at the Bible institute and speaking at the church every now and then, and I thought that was enough. But the Lord showed me it wasn't. Now, in Charlotte, my burden for souls intensified.

We can never outgrow our responsibility to witness. That's what God has called us all to do. And it's one of the highest callings in the world. All of us have a mandate to reap the vast harvest that is even now ripe in the fields around us. My reaping has taken me around the world many times over.

COMMITTED TO REMAIN SINGLE

During a prayer meeting one night, a pastor told me that God didn't want me to remarry. This was news to me. I was still young, and I was looking forward to marring some mighty man of God some day and ministering with him around the world. I could also see myself taking vacations and sailing the seas with such a consecrated and anointed companion. I asked the Lord if what this pastor had said was really His desire for me, and if it was, to tell me why. I went back to the prayer meeting a few weeks later, but before I went, I prayed and asked the Lord to show me His perfect will.

There were reports of tornados lurking around Charlotte that night, but I decided to weather the storm and go to prayer anyway. When I got there, it was announced that the prayer service would be canceled because many who normally attended from the surrounding areas had been unable to come. I was ready to turn around and go home, when the pastor said, "Let's have a word of prayer before everyone leaves."

TRIED IN THE FIRE

After we finished this prayer, he spoke to me individually. "The reason God has said He doesn't want you to marry again is that He has placed an apostolic anointing upon your life, and He doesn't want you to share that with a man." Well, that was a very different proposition. How could I say no to God.

Since I said my yes to God's will, doors have opened to me that only God could orchestrate. My mission trips have taken me to Portugal, Sweden, Switzerland, Holland, Denmark, Norway, Germany (three times), Spain, Morocco, Israel (twice), Guyana, Martinique, Barbados, Haiti, Puerto Rico (many times), the Antilles, Mexico, Curacao, St. Martins, St. Thomas, and Jamaica (many times).

I sailed the China seas, ate at the Great Hall of the People with Chinese dignitaries, climbed the Great Wall of China, and visited the cities of Hong Kong, Shanghai, Suzhou, Wenzhou, and Beijing.

I stood on Mars Hill in Athens, where the apostle Paul gave a powerful message on the local superstitions. I visited Nagasaki, Japan, Pusan, Korea, Quebec, Montreal, and Vancouver, in Canada, and places like Alaska and Hawaii, plus many great cities here in the United States.

And I haven't stopped yet. My latest trips were to Madrid Spain, and to Trinidad, West Indies. If the Lord delays His coming, I still have a desire to visit South Africa, Australia, New Zealand, Russia, the Philippines, and more. The Bible states emphatically:

GOD IS NOT UNRIGHTEOUS TO FORGET YOUR WORK

And this gospel of the kingdom shall be preached in all the world for a witness unto all nations; and then shall the end come.   Matthew 24:14

I must be an instrument in the hands of the Potter, to help get this Gospel out to all those who so desperately need it.

Chapter Sixteen

I Will Restore You to Health

*"For I will restore you to health
And I will heal you of your wounds," declares the* Lord,
*"Because they have called you an outcast, saying:
'It is Zion; no one cares for her.' "*

Jeremiah 30:17, NAS

Not long after Bishop passed away, I was in Memphis for the Convocation, and I began to experience some trouble with my eyes. I went to my sister's eye specialist, and he said he thought I had glaucoma and gave me some drops to put into my eyes.

A Healing Becomes a Healing Ministry

I started seeking God about it, and He led me not to use any of the drops. I knew then that He was about to heal me, without me having to use any medication. This began to increase my faith.

TRIED IN THE FIRE

The Lord had told me years before that He had given me the same anointing that He'd put on Kathryn Kuhlman, and if I spoke a word of healing to any sick person, He would heal them. I was afraid at the time, because seemingly everybody who lived in her day wanted her gift and anointing, and I thought that this was just a trick of my mind. I pondered it in my heart and kept living for the Lord, but I did nothing else about it.

One day Mother Lucille Laws said to me, "You know, you have the same gift that Kathryn Kuhlman has." I was shocked that God had revealed the same thing to her, and I asked Him how I should proceed. But, alas, I never launched out to operate in that anointing. Why does it take so much to cause us to be obedient to the calling of God?

It often seems that we're just waiting for the Lord to come down from Heaven and operate the gift Himself, when He wants to operate it through us. We must, at His word, let down the net, as the disciples were called upon to do. It doesn't matter if we've been fishing all night and have caught nothing. At His Word, we are to trust:

> *Trust and obey*
> *For there's no other way*
> *To be happy in Jesus,*
> *But to trust and obey.*

This seems difficult for many of us to do.

I WILL RESTORE YOU TO HEALTH

THE HEALING IS MANIFESTED

I believed God had healed my eyes, and one day I was watching Benny Hinn on television. At the end of his program, he started to pray for different kinds of illnesses. I said to the Lord, "If You have healed me, let him say that someone has been healed of glaucoma." No sooner had I prayed it than Benny Hinn said it. It was the confirmation I needed that God had done the work.

Many of us are still fleecing God, not being willing to believe, unless we first put out some fleece and have His answer to it. When I next went to Carolina Eye Clinic, to have my eyes examined, the doctor there checked me over and gave me a prescription for contact lenses. He also checked for glaucoma and told me that I didn't have any sign of it at all.

> *He had given me the same anointing that He'd put on Kathryn Kuhlman!*

I went again this past year, and the report was that my eyes were excellent. In fact, he said that my vision was actually stronger than the year before. I told him that my eyesight was very important to me because I was doing more and more work on computer. He said that I could do anything I wanted because my vision was fine. Praise the Lord! He is awesome!

TRIED IN THE FIRE

STARTING TO MINISTER HEALING

That was a breakthrough point for me, and I started ministering healing everywhere I traveled. In the process, I put together a list of all the healing scriptures in the Bible. (More on this in the next chapter.) I sent Dr. Faye Butler a copy, and her sister, Joy Walker, put it into a booklet form. I decided to design a booklet of my own and to give it out to all those who needed healing. This booklet has been instrumental in bringing healing to many, who are now believing God's Word. He said:

> *My son, give attention to my words;*
> *Incline your ear to my sayings.*
> *Do not let them depart from your sight;*
> *Keep them in the midst of your heart.*
> *For they are life to those who find them*
> *And health to all their body.*
> *Watch over your heart with all diligence,*
> *For from it flow the springs of life.*
> Proverbs 4:20-23, NAS

I have also included the healing scriptures as part of this book. Please concentrate on them. God says, *"Give attention to my words, for they are life to those who find them, and health to all their body."* What does this mean? It should be obvious.

I had been praying for many people suffering from high blood pressure, but when I went to my dentist to get a tooth pulled, he discovered that my pressure was very high and suggested that I might want to consult with my regular doctor. The truth was that I didn't even have a doctor at that point. I had been well for so long that I hadn't needed one.

WE HAVE A WORK TO DO

Saints, we have a work to do for the Lord, and we can't allow Satan to shut our bodies down. It is impossible for us to serve God in the grave. Therefore, we must put our faith and the Word of God into action now, while we still have breath. His Word declares:

> *Now faith is the assurance of things hoped for, the conviction of things not seen.* Hebrews 11:1, NAS

God's Word will never return unto Him void. It will accomplish what it says. As Jeremiah declared:

> *Then the LORD said to me, "You have seen well, for I am watching over My word to perform it."* Jeremiah 1:12, NAS

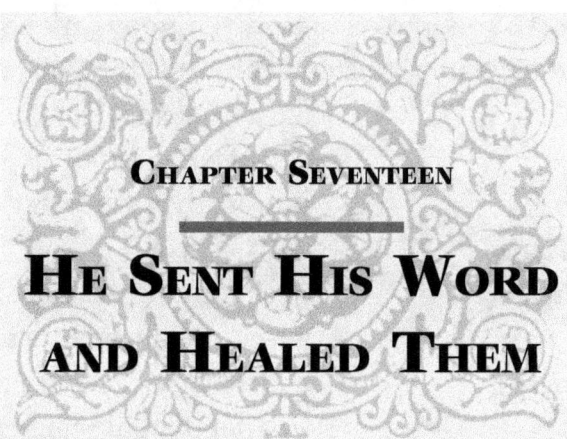

Chapter Seventeen

He Sent His Word and Healed Them

He sent His word and healed them,
And delivered them from their destructions.
Psalm 107:20, NAS

I'm convinced that many of the situations of life and the stresses produced by going through them contribute in a great way to our sicknesses. Because of this, being able to forgive and forget the painful side of our trials becomes vitally important. Indeed, it's a matter of life and death.

I woke up one morning, and could not move my arms and legs without severe pain. I called my prayer partner to agree in prayer with me, but I felt no immediate relief. I then called my daughter, who works in a medical office, and she made an appointment for me to visit Charlotte Orthopedic.

What's Wrong with Me?

The doctor assigned to me at the clinic administered a shot of cortisone into each arm. This gave me temporary relief, but after about fifteen minutes, the pain returned.

I was getting very concerned because I'd never experienced a pain that wouldn't go away with prayer.

> *I've always believed in seeking the Lord in fasting and prayer!*

I couldn't stoop to lie down without experiencing pain and had to buy an extra mattress, so that I could just roll over onto the bed. I couldn't sit down on a toilet seat and had to buy an ugly foam toilet seat that raised it up ten inches. I seemed to be getting worse.

I was referred to Carolina Medical Clinic for further observation. The doctors began to do tests, to come up with a logical diagnosis. In the meantime, friends who knew about my suffering suggested all sorts of remedies: two tablespoons of olive oil, apple cider vinegar, glucosamine, and chondroitin. For my part, I began to seriously seek the face of God. What was this? And could I expect to be like this the rest of my life?

Ministry from My Pastor

Superintendent Tommie Murphy, my pastor, has always been a supporter and encouragement to me, and one Sunday morning he called me out and asked a mother to come and lay hands on me while he prayed. I was so sure that this was the deliverance I'd been waiting for. I sank into that prayer and received every word of it. Still, during the next few days, I actually became worse.

Many times, when the mother saw me, she would ask me how I was feeling, and I would say something like, "I'm believing God," and she would say something like, "You just don't have enough faith." But, if that was the case, God could deal with that too.

There was a man in the Bible who confessed, *"Lord, I believe; help thou mine unbelief,"* (Mark 9:24), so it's okay to pray like that.

SEEKING THE LORD IN FASTING AND PRAYER

I've always believed in seeking the Lord in fasting and prayer, and the Holy Spirit brought to my remembrance what happened when Paul and Silas were in prison in Philippi:

> *But about midnight Paul and Silas were praying and singing hymns of praise to God, and the prisoners were listening to them; and suddenly there came a great earthquake, so that the foundations of the prison house were shaken; and immediately all the doors were opened and everyone's chains were unfastened.*
>
> Acts 16:25-26, NAS

TRIED IN THE FIRE

This sickness was a prison to me. I was bound by pain and misery and needed those chains to be loosed. I spoke to my pastor and asked if he and his wife would come to my house and pray with me and some of my close friends. Often, when praying past midnight, I've gotten real answers.

We began our prayer about 11:00 pm. Those present included Pastor and Mrs. Murphy, Rev. Carol Patterson (my sister), Pastor Regina Cherry, and her armorbearer, Sister Tina. They all started to seek God on my behalf, and then Pastor anointed my head with oil, and his wife anointed my body where the pain was. After midnight, knowing how busy and tired they must have been, I felt led to let them go home and rest.

My sister took up the prayer and prayed until she felt that she had prayed through. And then, she, too, left. Pastor Cherry and Sister Tina stayed on, praying with me through the night.

At some time in the wee hours of the morning, Pastor Cherry suggested that I should lie down and rest for a while. I consented, and in the serenity of the peace of God from the prayer, I heard a still small voice, saying to me, "I've seen your tears and heard your cry, and now I'm going to answer."

I was very excited and got up to tell the good news to the others. I was expecting that the pain would all be gone immediately, but it was only the beginning of the healing process. It would come in God's time.

People of God, don't be discouraged when healing or

blessing don't manifest themselves immediately. If God promised something, He will do it.

The Medical Diagnosis

I was still going to Carolina Medical Clinic, and they were sending me through all sorts of tests to determine what my problem was. Then the diagnosis came. I had rheumatoid arthritis, a crippling and painful disease.

My daughter Patricia, who worked in a medical office, mentioned to the drug reps that her mother was suffering from this thing, and they gave her some samples of Vioxx. Taking that gave me some relief from the pain, and in a few days, she brought something else to me. It was called Celebrex.

Celebrex was one of the most expensive drugs on the market, but her friends had sent me nearly a year's supply of it. I took it ... until it started to make me feel light-headed. I didn't like that feeling, so I stopped taking it.

The doctor at the clinic gave me a prescription for steroids, but when I noticed that those who had been taking it were gaining a lot of weight, I decided just to pray and believe God for my healing.

My Introduction to the Healing Scriptures

Then one day, on a televised ministry program, I heard a woman of God telling how her friend had been stricken with terminal cancer and was sent home to die. The sick lady and her husband, who was a pastor, began going through the Bible, picking out all the healing scriptures they could find. She read these over each night, and it brought

TRIED IN THE FIRE

her healing. She had now been cancer free for forty wonderful years.

When I heard that, I said to myself, "I need those scriptures." She said she would be giving half of them on Friday and the other half on the following Monday. I was determined not to miss either broadcast, and I watched and wrote down every scripture. I went on my computerized Bible program and made copies of each of those verses and then began reading them every night.

I heard a minister say that we need to speak to our sickness, and I began to prophesy to my joints.

I also involved myself with a televised exercise routine: ABLE, All Bodies Like Exercise. I gave my joints a workout every day and told them, "Joints, hear the Word of the Lord." I reminded them of what David had said:

I will praise thee; for I am fearfully and wonderfully made: marvellous are thy works; and that my soul knoweth right well. Psalm 139:14

"That's what I'm claiming," I declared.

THE RELEASE COMES

Two and a half weeks later, I was in church on a Wednesday night, and before he started his regular teaching, my pastor said, "I have a word for you." The word was from the prophet Habakkuk:

*Though the fig tree should not blossom
And there be no fruit on the vines,*

HE SENT HIS WORD AND HEALED THEM

Though the yield of the olive should fail
And the fields produce no food,
Though the flock should be cut off from the fold
And there be no cattle in the stalls,
Yet I will exult in the L ORD ,
I will rejoice in the God of my salvation.
*The Lord G*OD *is my strength,*
And He has made my feet like hinds' feet,
And makes me walk on my high places.
  Habakkuk 3:17-19, NAS

I jumped up off of my chair and started dancing on the feet that had been paining me for the past several months, and I've been dancing every since. God's Word is "powerful":

> *I jumped up off of my chair and started dancing!*

For the word of God is quick, and powerful, and sharper than any two-edged sword, piercing even to the dividing asunder of soul and spirit, and of the joints and marrow, and is a discerner of the thoughts and intents of the heart.   Hebrews 4:12

WHO IS YOUR BODY MECHANIC?

The Lord spoke to me one day and said, "If you had a

Cadillac and something happened to it, where would you take it?"

I answered, "To General Motors (meaning, back to the Cadillac dealership)."

He then said, "If you had a Mercedes, would you take it to a corner mechanic?"

I said, "No, Lord. It would cost me more after he had finished with it, because he doesn't know how to work on that car."

Then the Lord said to me, "Then, why don't people bring their bodies back to Me? I made the body; shouldn't I know more about the body than doctors?"

Yes, God has given us doctors, but we should, at the very least, ask Him first if and where we should go for medical attention, which doctor He recommends for us, and what He does and doesn't want us to take in the way of medication. He will lead and guide us in all things.

When Afflictions Come

I thought, after being healed from that sickness, that I would be well the rest of my life, but afflictions come to us down here on this earth:

> *Many are the afflictions of the righteous,*
> *But the* Lord *delivers him out of them all.*
> Psalm 34:19, NAS

Each time I am afflicted in any way, I look to Him who delivers, and He never fails me.

Chapter Eighteen
With His Stripes We Are Healed

Surely he hath borne our griefs, and carried our sorrows: yet we did esteem him stricken, smitten of God, and afflicted. But he was wounded for our transgressions, he was bruised for our iniquities: the chastisement of our peace was upon him; and with his stripes we are healed.   Isaiah 53:4-5

Several mornings I awoke with hot, fiery pains in my body, and I had developed a serious looking rash. I once again spoke to Patricia, who has become like the doctor in our family. She is now very talented when it comes to giving diagnoses and prescribing medication, although she is not a doctor. She just happened to be off from work that morning and came over to take me to see her doctor. All the while, I was asking the Lord, "Why am I going through this again?"

TRIED IN THE FIRE

SHINGLES

After the doctor examined me, he still wasn't sure what I had. "I think maybe you just broke out from something," he said.

But Patricia said, "Doctor, doesn't this look like shingles?" He had to admit that it did and called in a lady dermatologist to take a look. She looked at the "rash" through her magnifying glass and decided that, yes, it was shingles. The doctor prescribed something for me, but even with that, I still suffered a lot of pain, the kind you can't sleep with.

As I understand it, shingles is a virus that affects your nerve endings, and it's difficult to get anything down there deep enough to treat it.

MY PROMISE TO WRITE A BOOK

I questioned the Lord, wanting to know why this was happening. He reminded me that I had been promising to write a book that would help others who were facing similar tests in life, and I hadn't yet gotten started on it. If this severe pain wouldn't get me moving on it, nothing would.

I felt like Jonah, who suffered for his unwillingness to go to Ninevah, and then, when he had begun his journey, he got there in record time. I sat down and started to write, and in no time at all, my book was complete. No sooner had I begun to write than I was finishing up this final chapter.

WITH HIS STRIPES WE ARE HEALED

HEALED IN RECORD TIME

I was very happy that my case of shingles had not been as severe as some. With some people, it affects the entire body. By reading the Word of God and speaking to my sickness, mine were cleared up in record time.

I thank God for His merciful kindness to me through the years, and I dedicate myself to always be obedient to His every desire in the future.

The Healing Scriptures

Dear reader, the following Bible verses have been compiled to help you appropriate the power in the Word of God for your life and for your healing. Because Jesus is the Word, we have life and healing through His name:

In the beginning was the Word, and the Word was with God, and the Word was God. John 1:1

He cast out the spirits with his word, and healed all that were sick. Matthew 8:16

So, Read the Word,

        Speak the Word,

                Agree with the Word,

AND BE HEALED!

TRIED IN THE FIRE

Isaiah 54:10, NAS:
> "For the mountains may be removed and the hills may shake,
> But My lovingkindness will not be removed from you,
> And My covenant of peace will not be shaken,"
> Says the Lord who has compassion on you.

Exodus 15:26, NAS:
> And He said, "If you will give earnest heed to the voice of the Lord your God, and do what is right in His sight, and give ear to His commandments, and keep all His statutes, I will put none of the diseases on you which I have put on the Egyptians; for I, the Lord, am your healer."

Exodus 23:25, NAS:
> But you shall serve the Lord your God, and He will bless your bread and your water; and I will remove sickness from your midst.

Deuteronomy 7:15, NAS:
> The Lord will remove from you all sickness; and He will not put on you any of the harmful diseases of Egypt which you have known, but He will lay them on all who hate you.

Deuteronomy 28:1-14, NAS:
> Now it shall be, if you diligently obey the Lord

your God, being careful to do all His commandments which I command you today, the L*ORD your God will set you high above all the nations of the earth. All these blessings will come upon you and overtake you if you obey the* L*ORD your God: Blessed shall you be in the city, and blessed shall you be in the country. Blessed shall be the offspring of your body and the produce of your ground and the offspring of your beasts, the increase of your herd and the young of your flock. Blessed shall be your basket and your kneading bowl. Blessed shall you be when you come in, and blessed shall you be when you go out. The* L*ORD shall cause your enemies who rise up against you to be defeated before you; they will come out against you one way and will flee before you seven ways. The* L*ORD will command the blessing upon you in your barns and in all that you put your hand to, and He will bless you in the land which the* L*ORD your God gives you. The* L*ORD will establish you as a holy people to Himself, as He swore to you, if you keep the commandments of the* L*ORD your God and walk in His ways. So all the peoples of the earth will see that you are called by the name of the* L*ORD, and they will be afraid of you. The* L*ORD will make you abound in prosperity, in the offspring of your body and in the offspring of your beast and in the produce of your* *ground, in the land which the LORD swore to your fathers to give you. The LORD will open for you His good storehouse, the heavens, to give rain to your land in its season and to bless all the work of your hand; and you shall lend to many nations, but you shall not borrow. The LORD will make you the head and not the tail, and you only will be above, and you will not be underneath, if you listen to the commandments of the LORD your God, which I charge you today, to observe them carefully, and do not turn aside from any of the words which I command you today, to the right or to the left, to go after other gods to serve them.*

Deuteronomy 30:19-20, NAS:

I call heaven and earth to witness against you today, that I have set before you life and death, the blessing and the curse. So choose life in order that you may live, you and your descendants, by loving the LORD your God, by obeying His voice, and by holding fast to Him; for this is your life and the length of your days, that you may live in the land which the LORD swore to your fathers, to Abraham, Isaac, and Jacob, to give them.

Proverbs 10:7, NAS:

The memory of the righteous is blessed.

THE HEALING SCRIPTURES

1 Peter 1:13, NAS:
Therefore, prepare your minds for action, keep sober in spirit, fix your hope completely on the grace to be brought to you at the revelation of Jesus Christ.

Hebrews 10:35-36, NAS:
Therefore, do not throw away your confidence, which has a great reward. For you have need of endurance, so that when you have done the will of God, you may receive what was promised.

Hebrews 11:1, NAS:
Now faith is the assurance of things hoped for, the conviction of things not seen.

Hebrews 13:8, NAS:
Jesus Christ is the same yesterday and today and forever.

James 5:13-15, NAS:
Is anyone among you suffering? Then he must pray. Is anyone cheerful? He is to sing praises. Is anyone among you sick? Then he must call for the elders of the church and they are to pray over him, anointing him with oil in the name of the Lord; and the prayer offered in faith will restore the one who is sick, and the Lord will raise him

up, and if he has committed sins, they will be forgiven him.

1 Peter 2:24, NAS:
And He Himself bore our sins in His body on the cross, so that we might die to sin and live to righteousness; for by His wounds you were healed.

3 John 1:2, NAS:
Beloved, I pray that in all respects you may prosper and be in good health, just as your soul prospers.

1 John 3:20-22, NAS:
In whatever our heart condemns us; for God is greater than our heart and knows all things. Beloved, if our heart does not condemn us, we have confidence before God; and whatever we ask we receive from Him, because we keep His commandments and do the things that are pleasing in His sight.

1 John 5:14-15, NAS:
This is the confidence which we have before Him, that, if we ask anything according to His will, He hears us. And if we know that He hears us in whatever we ask, we know that we have the requests which we have asked from Him.

THE HEALING SCRIPTURES

2 Timothy 1:7, NAS:
For God has not given us a spirit of timidity, but of power and love and discipline.

Ephesians 6:10-18, NAS:
Finally, be strong in the Lord and in the strength of His might. Put on the full armor of God, so that you will be able to stand firm against the schemes of the devil. For our struggle is not against flesh and blood, but against the rulers, against the powers, against the world forces of this darkness, against the spiritual forces of wickedness in the heavenly places. Therefore, take up the full armor of God, so that you will be able to resist in the evil day, and having done everything, to stand firm. Stand firm therefore, HAVING GIRDED YOUR LOINS WITH TRUTH and HAVING PUT ON THE BREASTPLATE OF RIGHTEOUSNESS, and having shod YOUR FEET WITH THE PREPARATION OF THE GOSPEL OF PEACE; in addition to all, taking up the shield of faith with which you will be able to extinguish all the flaming arrows of the evil one. And take THE HELMET OF SALVATION, and the sword of the Spirit, which is the word of God. With all prayer and petition pray at all times in the Spirit, and with this in view, be on the alert with all perseverance and petition for all the saints.

TRIED IN THE FIRE

Philippians 2:13, NAS:
> *For it is God who is at work in you, both to will and to work for His good pleasure.*

Philippians 4:4-8, NAS:
> *Rejoice in the Lord always; again I will say, rejoice! Let your gentle spirit be known to all men. The Lord is near. Be anxious for nothing, but in everything by prayer and supplication with thanksgiving let your requests be made known to God. And the peace of God, which surpasses all comprehension, will guard your hearts and your minds in Christ Jesus. Finally, brethren, whatever is true, whatever is honorable, whatever is right, whatever is pure, whatever is lovely, whatever is of good repute, if there is any excellence and if anything worthy of praise, dwell on these things.*

Hebrews 10:23, NAS:
> *Let us hold fast the confession of our hope without wavering, for He who promised is faithful.*

1 Kings 8:56, NAS:
> *Blessed be the LORD, who has given rest to His people Israel, according to all that He promised ; not one word has failed of all His good promise, which He promised through Moses His servant.*

THE HEALING SCRIPTURES

Psalm 107:20, NAS:
> He sent His word and healed them,
> And delivered them from their destructions.

Psalm 118:17, NAS:
> I will not die, but live,
> And tell of the works of the Lord.

Proverbs 4:20-23, NAS:
> My son, give attention to my words;
> Incline your ear to my sayings.
> Do not let them depart from your sight;
> Keep them in the midst of your heart.
> For they are life to those who find them
> And health to all their body.
> Watch over your heart with all diligence,
> For from it flow the springs of life.

Isaiah 41:10, NAS:
> Do not fear, for I am with you;
> Do not anxiously look about you, for I am your God.
> I will strengthen you, surely I will help you,
> Surely I will uphold you with My righteous right hand.

Isaiah 53:4-5, NAS:
> Surely our griefs He Himself bore,
> And our sorrows He carried;
> Yet we ourselves esteemed Him stricken,

TRIED IN THE FIRE

Smitten of God, and afflicted.
But He was pierced through for our transgressions,
He was crushed for our iniquities;
The chastening for our well-being fell upon Him,
And by His scourging we are healed.

Jeremiah 1:12, NAS:
Then the Lord said to me, "You have seen well, for I am watching over My word to perform it."

Jeremiah 30:17, NAS:
"For I will restore you to health
And I will heal you of your wounds," declares the Lord, "Because they have called you an outcast, saying:
'It is Zion; no one cares for her.'"

Joel 3:10, NAS:
Beat your plowshares into swords
And your pruning hooks into spears;
Let the weak say, "I am a mighty man."

Nahum 1:9, NAS:
Whatever you devise against the Lord,
He will make a complete end of it.
Distress will not rise up twice.

Matthew 8:2-3, NAS:
And a leper came to Him and bowed down be-

fore Him, and said, "Lord, if You are willing, You can make me clean." Jesus stretched out His hand and touched him, saying, "I am willing; be cleansed." And immediately his leprosy was cleansed.

Matthew 18:18-20, NAS:
Truly I say to you, whatever you bind on earth shall have been bound in heaven; and whatever you loose on earth shall have been loosed in heaven. Again I say to you, that if two of you agree on earth about anything that they may ask, it shall be done for them by My Father who is in heaven. For where two or three have gathered together in My name, I am there in their midst.

Matthew 21:21, NAS:
And Jesus answered and said to them, "Truly I say to you, if you have faith and do not doubt, you will not only do what was done to the fig tree, but even if you say to this mountain, 'Be taken up and cast into the sea,' it will happen."

Mark 11:23, NAS:
Truly I say to you, whoever says to this mountain, "Be taken up and cast into the sea," and does not doubt in his heart, but believes that what he says is going to happen, it will be granted him.

TRIED IN THE FIRE

Mark 16:17-18, NAS:
> These signs will accompany those who have believed: in My name they will cast out demons, they will speak with new tongues; they will pick up serpents, and if they drink any deadly poison, it will not hurt them; they will lay hands on the sick, and they will recover.

Ezekiel 16:6, NAS:
> When I passed by you and saw you squirming in your blood, I said to you while you were in your blood, "Live!" Yes, I said to you while you were in your blood, "Live!"

John 10:10, NAS:
> The thief comes only to steal and kill and destroy; I came that they may have life, and have it abundantly.

Romans 4:17-21, NAS:
> (As it is written, "A FATHER OF MANY NATIONS HAVE I MADE YOU") in the presence of Him whom he believed, even God, who gives life to the dead and calls into being that which does not exist. In hope against hope he believed, so that he might become a father of many nations according to that which had been spoken, "SO SHALL YOUR DESCENDANTS BE." Without becoming weak in faith he contemplated his own

body, now as good as dead since he was about a hundred years old, and the deadness of Sarah's womb; yet, with respect to the promise of God, he did not waver in unbelief but grew strong in faith, giving glory to God, and being fully assured that what God had promised, He was able also to perform.

Romans 8:11, NAS:
But if the Spirit of Him who raised Jesus from the dead dwells in you, He who raised Christ Jesus from the dead will also give life to your mortal bodies through His Spirit who dwells in you.

2 Corinthians 10:4-5, NAS:
For the weapons of our warfare are not of the flesh, but divinely powerful for the destruction of fortresses. We are destroying speculations and every lofty thing raised up against the knowledge of God, and we are taking every thought captive to the obedience of Christ.

Galatians 3:13-14, NAS:
Christ redeemed us from the curse of the Law, having become a curse for us—for it is written, "CURSED IS EVERYONE WHO HANGS ON A TREE" in order that in Christ Jesus the blessing of Abraham might come to the Gentiles, so that we would receive the promise of the Spirit through faith.

NOTES

You may contact the author at:

*G.L. Washington Ministry
P.O. Box 667444
Charlotte, NC 28266*

Telephone: *(800) 484-6586*
Email: *contact@drgwendolynwashington.com*
www.drgwendolynwashington.com

www.ingramcontent.com/pod-product-compliance
Lightning Source LLC
LaVergne TN
LVHW051549070426
835507LV00021B/2481